U0896899

Sunshine Chinese
Teachers' Guidebook 2

阳光汉语教师手册

主　编　刘　骏〔美〕
(Jun Liu)

2013年 • 北京

主　　编：Jun Liu〔美〕

编　　者：魏慧萍

英文审订：梅　皓

Preface

As we all know, there are two critical factors affecting the learning of a foreign language. One is the environment in which learners are exposed to the language in its cultural surroundings and they can pick up the language and use it on almost all occasions because the society functions in that language. The other is the age of learning a language, with or without the language environment. It is a common belief that the earlier learners start acquiring a foreign language, the better they will learn as a result. Many studies on younger learners' learning of foreign languages suggest that there is a "critical period." Children who start learning a foreign language before the age of 13 or 14 are able to acquire pronunciation and intonation of that language more naturally.Correct pronunciation and intonation will, in return, help learn vocabulary, ease communication, and boost self-confidence.

There are many success stories about early learning of a foreign language, such as Canadian early immersion programs and bilingual programs in many US elementary schools. But there are few examples of successful learning of Chinese as a foreign language for children, especially younger children. Apart from the lack of sufficient teachers, effective methodology and comprehensive curricula, a major reason is the lack of age-appropriate materials that are fun-filled, quick to learn, and easy to assess.

As such, we have designed and developed our Chinese for Youth series titled "Sunshine Chinese" that caters to elementary and junior high students as they develop the basic communicative competence in Chinese language. This series is the first attempt to align the vocabulary and language functions with the Youth Chinese Test (YCT) developed by Hanban (Office of Chinese Language Teaching International). This YCT-friendly textbook series will greatly assist learners with self-assessment and provide needed feedback for teachers to understand their learners' learning outcome unit after unit and book after book in the series. The theme story, which weaves through the entire series of four textbooks, is contextualized in an international school in China where children from all parts of the world are befriended in a multicultural and supportive environment. Our rationale for Sunshine Chinese is: Experience Chinese, Understand China, and Appreciate the World.

It has taken an entire team's dedication to this project for the last couple of years. As series editor, I would first and foremost thank the leadership of the Commercial Press, Duputy Director Dr. Hongbo Zhou whose insight, determination, and steady support have been impeccable. I would give my special thanks to Yueyan Liu whose continuous engagement, high responsibility, and seamless coordination have made this series possible. My sincere gratitude and appreciation also go to the entire team: Dr. Huiping Wei, Professor Xiuqing Wang, Master Teacher Wen Yi, Dr. Yuemei Wu, and Professor Yanfeng Zhao for their expertise, experience, and great synergies in shaping and reshaping the textbooks in this series. As the characters grow in the series, so do our authors' confidence, enthusiasm, and expectations.

As the Vice President of the International Society of Chinese Language Teaching (ISCLT), senior consultant of Hanban, former Director of Confucius Institute at the University of Arizona, and current Associate Provost for International Initiatives at Georgia State University, I am excited about this first-ever YCT-friendly book series. I sincerely hope that this series will be adopted by as many schools as possible. Through the feedback and input, we, together, will make this series better as the next generation of multilingual talents develop to make this world a better place for us all.

Jun Liu

Editor, Sunshine Chinese Series

TABLE OF CONTENTS

How to Use This Book

The teacher's guide book is designed to go with the "Sunshine Chinese" textbooks, providing helpful teaching resources and skills to combine Chinese teaching with the Youth Chinese Test (YCT) in an available way.

There are 4 main parts in the lesson plan of each unit: Lesson objectives, Target Vocabulary and Sentence Structure, Suggested Activities and Assessment.

Lesson objectives comprise *language* and *culture*. Language objectives provides concise and specific description of the functions students are expected to grasp, while cultural items aspects tied to the storyline and language points in each unit.

We specially encourage the teachers present the cultural items as vividly as possible. Some of them are really practical and interesting, such as why Chinese people hung "福" upside down, how to use the Chinese brush and so on. We also try to give the picture of some real scenes in China today, such as the international schools, the one-child families, and some beautiful cities in China.

Target Vocabulary and Sentence Structure lists the vocabulary items and sentence structures that are the foci of each unit and on which students will be assessed. These items and structures are tied to YCT framework totally.

We also provide few additional words or expressions when needed in some teaching tips, allowing teachers to select according to students' level and interests.

Suggested Activities play a major part in this guidebook, with a large variety of activities including games, songs, projects for classroom and out of school settings as well.

In this part, the role of the teacher is emphasized in Guided Practice, which needs the teacher lead students in pronunciation and comprehension as well. Some useful and fun games are provided, such as Character cards game, Fly swatters, Teacher versus students, Observe and judge, Listen and match , Trace and say, and so forth.

In Independent Practice, we encourage learners to build self-confidence and productive competence in Chinese. The activities spur students on to use Chinese language more positively and get integrated skills including listening, speaking, reading and writing, such as Whispers, Get the ball and answer my question, Free talking, Characters-words-sentences, Perform a script, My storybook, Survey, Let's sing, and so forth.

To avoid repetition, for frequently used games or activities, a clear explanation is provided as ***Appendix*** of this book. The instructions are also provided when the games or activities appear for the first time.

We suggest the teachers set up pairs or groups from the very beginning of Chinese class to encourage students learn from each other. It's also necessary to re-arrange the pairs or groups after a certain period in order to develop students' interactive skills. The teacher can pick activities from the Suggested Activities and choose the ones that are best suited to their students' age, levels and needs.

For the sake of convenience, the worksheets are provided in the students' Workbook. These activities with the worksheets available in the Workbook are marked with "Workbook".

Assessment covers the new language items in the units, including tools for assessment of listening, speaking and reading. Some of them are designed with YCT model and the others in more flexible way.

The Mid-term test (testing Units1–6) and the final test (testing Units1–12) are provided in the end of this guidebook. These two tests offer a good sample for teachers and students to get familiarized with YCT in terms of its content, style and difficulty, as well as a tool for teaching and learning evaluation.

A MP3 is provided with rich teaching samples, for example, songs from the Workbook, texts reading, text slide show, and YCT-Friendly tests.

We hope this guidebook will help the teachers to find the suitable approach of teaching Chinese as a foreign language for children and to create joyful overseas Chinese classes as well.

UNIT 1

我的名字叫王贝贝

LESSON OBJECTIVES

Language

Students will be able to

- Introduce themselves with basic information.
- Use the 的 phrase.
- Use the adverb 也.

Culture

Students will know about

- Common Chinese boys' and girls' names.

  Some common Chinese names:

  For boys: 军(army) 强(strong) 伟(great)

  For girls: 丽(beautiful) 怡(happy) 芳(fragrant)

  Chinese parents consider good names very important for their children, so they're inclined to convey their wishes for their children through the meanings of characters in their names.

- The pictographic nature of the Chinese characters.

  Modern Chinese characters still retain pictographic elements which are inherited from ancient Chinese characters. You may find some characters appear like pictures. Here are some interesting examples:

月

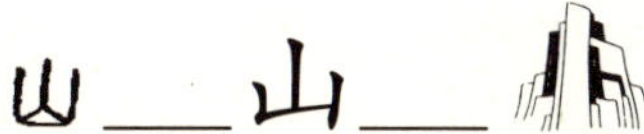

人

TEACHING TIP

The teacher should choose the proper time to introduce these cultural points. They can be tied to the practice exercises in the workbook or related to the pictures which present similar points on the textbook. The teacher can also design some games to practice the cultural points more. For example: Encourage students to guess the meanings of some simple Chinese characters, such as 大, 木, 明, 雨, and so on.

TARGET VOCABULARY AND SENTENCE STRUCTURE

Vocabulary

名字	今年	了	学生
小学生	北京	医院	也

Sentence Structure

我的名字叫（name）。
我的爸爸是（occupation）。
Pronoun / Noun 也+Verb

SUGGESTED ACTIVITIES

Guided Practice

- 字卡游戏 Character Cards Game

  The teacher prepares the character cards for this lesson and demonstrates the correct words with these cards while reading the words. The teacher gives students 5-8 minutes to remember the words. The words are presented in two columns, one is a monosyllabic word and the other is a two-syllable word.

  也　了　名字　今年　北京　医生　学生

  Then shuffle the cards. Students should try to get all of the words with the character cards. The group who can get more right words will be the winner.

- 拍词游戏 Fly Swatters

  The teacher prepares a visual of the vocabulary pictures. Students are divided into two teams and line up in two lines. The first person in each line has a fly swatter. Then the teacher says one vocabulary item, the person who hits the visual first wins one point for the team.

- 师生竞赛 Teacher versus Students

  The teacher prepares a visual of the vocabulary pictures. When the teacher points to a picture and says the correct word in Chinese, all the students should "chorally" repeat the word. If the teacher says the wrong word in Chinese, all the students should remain silent. If all the students remain silent when the teacher is "wrong", they receive a point. If any student starts to repeat the wrong word, the teacher receives the point.

- 连一连 Match **Workbook**

  Match the Chinese sentences to the right pictures.

  The teacher leads students, reading the sentences while they matching them to the pictures.

- 中文名字 Chinese Name **Workbook**

  Write down your own Chinese name with your teacher's help and try to understand its meaning, and then talk about it with your partner.

  The teacher should prepare a list of Chinese names for the students, then, give brief explanations of the meanings of common Chinese names. For instance：

丽 means beautiful	怡 means happy	宝 means treasure
伟 means great	强 means strong	华 means China

TEACHING TIP

The teacher should give necessary guidance while students are talking about their Chinese names in pairs.

- 边写边说 Let's Trace and Say **Workbook**

  Prepare some flashcards to introduce the pictographic nature of Chinese characters, taking 日 and 月 as examples, then help students to trace these two characters in the correct stroke order.

- 你的家在哪里 Where's Your Home **Workbook**

  Have students paste the pictures of where they are from in the workbook. Lead students in reading some new words that appear here (such as 纽约, 悉尼, 首尔), then provide students the Chinese name of the local city.

- 选图片 Listen and Circle **Workbook**
  Circle the pictures corresponding to what the teacher says.
  Read the following sentences for twice while asking students to circle the corresponding pictures.
  1. 爸爸是医生。
  2. 妈妈是老师。
  3. 哥哥是学生。
  4. 姐姐也是学生。

- 自我介绍 Self-introduction **Workbook**
  Introduce yourself in the light of the example. Practice with your partner first, then choose your lucky number from your teacher's number box. The students who get 3 or the multiples of 3 will give self-introduction in Chinese before the class.
  The teacher provides some new words such as 商人 and 家庭主妇. More words about career related to this practice can be added if the students want to learn more.

> **TEACHING TIP**
> The teacher prepares a number box. Let each student choose a number from the box in several times (10 students for one time). The lucky students who get 3, 6 or 9 will introduce themselves before the class.

Independent Practice

- 我是谁 Who am I
  Ask for a volunteer to say some information about himself/herself while standing behind the class, so that other students can't see him/her while guessing his/her name. The person who guesses correctly will take the role of the volunteer and continue to play this game. One should give more information in the form of Chinese sentences if the others can't guess his/her name.

- 字—词—句 Characters—words—sentences
  Divide the class in groups, each group including 5 students at least. Everyone gets a character card and should find the others to assemble words and sentences quickly. The group which forms most words and sentences will be the winner. The winner should present the words and sentences by standing in a row while holding the cards in the correct order.

- 接球问答 Get the Ball and Answer My Question

  Throw a soft ball to some student. After the student catches the ball, ask some questions.

  Suggested questions:

  你叫什么名字？/你今年几岁了？/你的家在哪里？/你是小学生吗？/你的爸爸是医生吗？/你的妈妈是老师吗？

  Students who can answer the questions in Chinese correctly and quickly will earn the chance to throw the ball and ask others.

- 耳语 Whispers

  Students are required to convey a whispered message one by one in order to convey a sentence which the teacher says to the first person in each line.

  Step1：Group the students into teams and ask them stand in lines.
  Step2：Whisper to the first student in each line:
  我的名字叫（the true name of the teacher）。
  我今年二十岁。
  Tom喜欢汉语，我也喜欢汉语。
  李心爱的妈妈不是老师。
  王贝贝的家在北京。
  Step3：Students whisper the sentence to the student behind them.
  Step4：The last student in each line speaks the sentence aloud.

  The team that ends up with the exact sentence wins this game.

- 我的名片 My Name Card

  Ask students to make their name cards based on the sample. Then exchange name cards with their friends in class.

姓名Name	男Boy 女Girl
国籍Nationality	年龄Age
职业Career	爱好Hobby

- 年龄调查 A Survey of Birth Date and Age **Workbook**
  Ask students to do a survey of the birth date and age of family members in Chinese and draw the birthday gifts they like.

- 唱一唱 Let's Sing **Workbook**
  Lead students in practicing this song in pairs and groups. Then encourage students to replace Beibei's information with their real information. Ask two students to perform the dialogues appear in the beginning and the end of this song.

♪♫ 贝贝之歌♪♫

贝贝！你好！你好！
我的名字叫贝贝，你的名字叫什么？
我今年九岁了，你今年几岁呀？
我的家在北京，你的家在哪里？
我的爸爸是医生，妈妈是老师。
我的名字叫贝贝，你的名字叫什么？
我今年九岁了，你今年几岁呀？
我的家在北京，你的家在哪里？
我是一个学生。一个小学生，一个小学生。
贝贝！再见，再见！

Question for Reflection

What's your first impression of Chinese characters?

TEACHING TIP

The teacher encourages students talk about the question in groups. Then, each group gets a representative to declare their ideas. At last, the teacher gives a summary with some common characteristics of Chinese characters.

ASSESSMENT

Listening

选择图片

Choose the pictures corresponding to the dialogues you have heard twice.

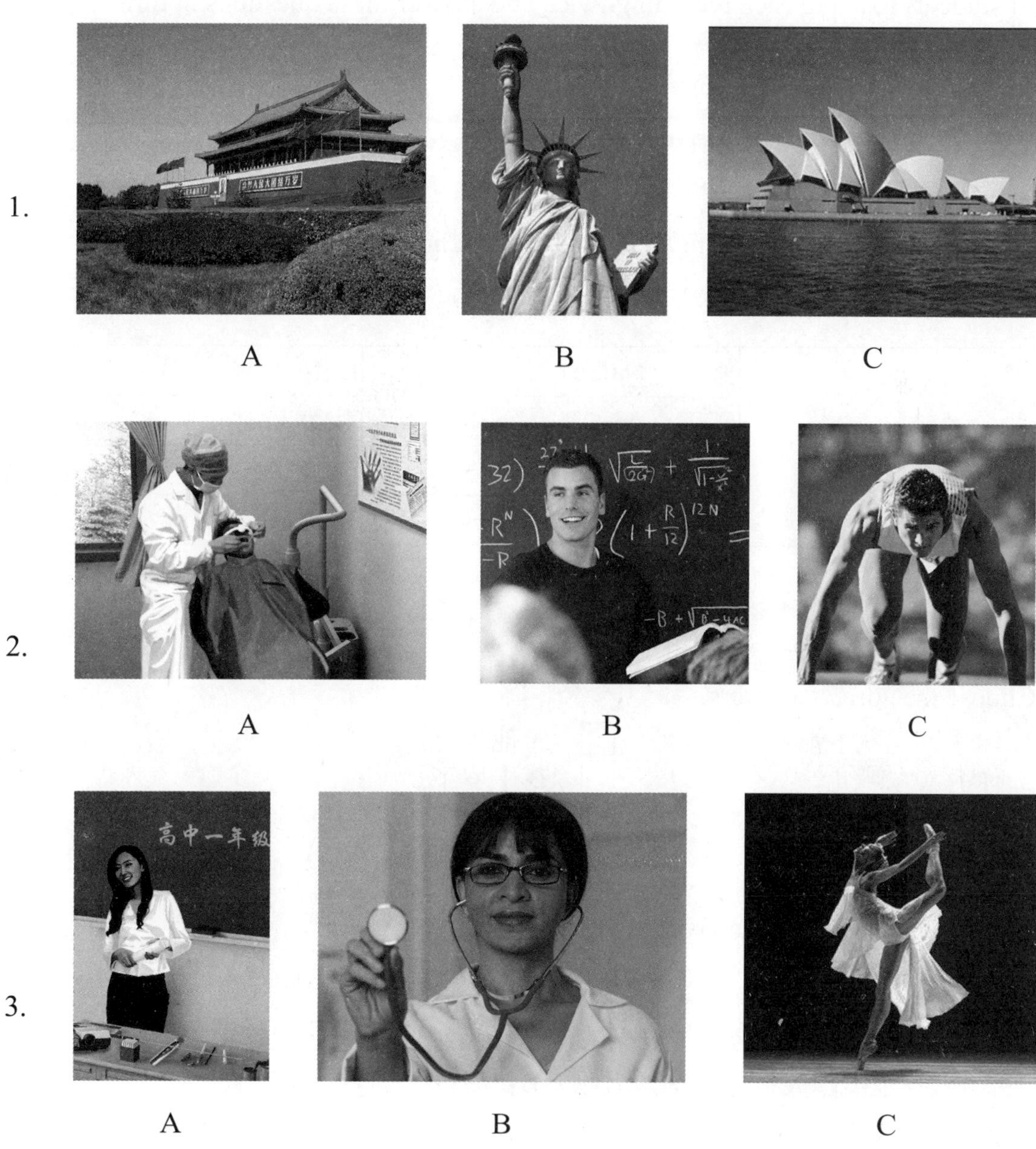

选择答案

Choose the correct answers to the questions you have heard twice.

4. (　) A 我有一个哥哥。　B 我的家在美国。　C 我喜欢我的老师。

5. (　) A 李心爱是韩国人。 B 李心爱也是小学生。 C 李心爱今年十一岁。
6. (　) A 我爸爸很好。 B 我妈妈是老师。 C 我爸爸是医生。

Speaking

听后回答

Prepare a recording of the self-introductions of a few students (3-5 will suffice), then let students listen to each recording twice and answer these questions in turn.

1. 他/她叫什么名字?
2. 他/她今年几岁了?
3. 他的家在哪儿?

看图说话

Describe the person appearing in the picture in Chinese.

Prepare some resume forms. For example:

	姓名 (Name)	Kate
	年龄 (Age)	12岁
	国籍 (Nationality)	美国
	职业 (Career)	学生

Reading

选择答案

Choose the correct answers.

1. 你今年几岁了? ☐ A 他也是。
2. 你的家在哪儿? ☐ B 十岁了。
3. 他也是中国人吗? ☐ C 在北京。

选词填空

Fill in the blanks with the given words.

A 也　　B 了　　C 名字

4. A：你叫什么(　　)? B：我叫王小月。
5. A：你几岁? B：我今年十二岁(　　)。
6. A：我是美国人，你是美国人吗? B：我(　　)是美国人。

Free Reading

Independent Practice "My name card" can be used as a rubric for assessment here. Ask students exchange their name cards in pairs and read the information on the cards, then take turns telling the teacher what they read on the cards.

UNIT 2

新同学

LESSON OBJECTIVES

Language

Students will be able to

- Introduce others with basic information.
- Use 哪 to pose questions.
- Use some courteous phrases in Chinese.

Culture

Students will know about

- General polite phrases in Chinese.
  Chinese people add 请 before the verbs to express respect.
  For example: 请坐,请看,请喝. However, the persons who have a very close relationship seldom use 请 in their conversations as it would feel unnatural.
  The common sentence to express appreciation is 谢谢你. The proper answer is 不客气.
  A brief apology can be made in Chinese with the phrase 对不起. One who accepts the apology will answer with 没关系 to show "it doesn't matter".

- The differences between greetings in different countries.

People have different customs to greet each other in different countries. Modern Chinese people shake hands or nod to each other while Americans give hugs to each other. In Japan and Korea, people have carried on their traditional form of greeting, bowing to each other, especially to the elders and superiors.

If possible, provide show slides to illustrate the differences. Some useful pictures could be found in films.

TARGET VOCABULARY AND SENTENCE STRUCTURE

Vocabulary

新　　同学　　请　　坐　　对不起

没关系　　日本　　不客气　　好吃

Notice：新 appears in level 3 of YCT. 日本 is an additional word here.

Sentence Structure

1. 你是哪国人?
2. 认识你很高兴。
3. 对不起。/ 没关系。
4. 谢谢你。/ 不客气。

SUGGESTED ACTIVITIES

Guided Practice

- 字卡游戏 Character Cards Game

  The teacher can present the words in three columns: they are monosyllabic words, two-syllable words and three-syllable words.

  新　请　坐

  同学　日本

  对不起　没关系　不客气

- 拍词游戏 Fly Swatters

- 师生竞赛 Teacher versus Students

- 连一连 Match **Workbook**
  Match the Chinese sentences to the right pictures.The teacher leads students in reading the sentences.

- 你是哪国人 Where Are You From **Workbook**
  Choose the corresponding description for each person. Help students to choose and lead them in reading the dialogues.

- 观察与判断 Observe and Judge **Workbook**
  Determine nationalities of the people according to their performances in the pictures.

> **TEACHING TIP**
> The teacher explains greetings in the U.S.A., China and Japan or Korea, such as hugging, shaking hands and bowing. Find some interesting videos if possible.

- 写写说说 Let's Trace and Say **Workbook**
  Prepare some flashcards to present the structure and the right stroke order of 田. Then encourage students to write and read it.

- 听听连连 Listen and Match **Workbook**
  The teacher should read the sentences twice,than ask the students to match the right pictures to the right sentences.

- 介绍新同学 Introduce a New Classmate **Workbook**
  Choose a classmate as a newcomer to the Chinese class. Then introduce him/her in the format of the example. Practice with your partner first, then choose a number from your teacher's number box. The students who get 5 or a multiple of 5 will give the introduction in Chinese before the class.

> **TEACHING TIP**
> The teacher prepares a number box and lets each student choose a number from the box (10 students at a time). The lucky students who get 5 or 10 will present introduction before the class.

Independent Practice

- 西蒙说 Simon Says
  The teacher should find a volunteer to begin this game with the sentences:

(   ) 同学，请坐！
Simon 说，(   ) 同学，请坐！
The person who hears his/her name in the second sentence should sit down immediately and continue to play the game. One can't say the name of a classmate who's already sat down. Ones who sit down when they heard the first sentence (without "Simon 说") will be "out".

- 字—词—句 Characters—words—sentences

- 耳语 Whispers
  The teacher whispers to the first student of each line:
  谢谢你！/不客气。/对不起。/没关系。/认识你很高兴。/我也很高兴。

- 我的心情卡片 My Feeling Card
  Do you want to say "thanks" to someone? Or you really want to say "sorry" to someone for some particular reason? Do it now! Make a beautiful card to express your feelings and write the Chinese sentences 谢谢你 or 对不起 on your card.

- 课本剧表演 Perform a Script
  Put three students in one group. Act out the script. After practicing, perform in turn and choose the best team. Encourage students to imagine various situations of the text and perform freely.

- 唱一唱 Let's Sing **Workbook**
  Practice this song in pairs. Then divide the whole class into two groups and practice it again.Ask students sing this song in different roles.

♪♫ 新同学 ♪♫

新同学，新同学，谁是新同学？
这是我们的新同学，新呀新同学。
你好!新同学。认识你很高兴。
我也很高兴。我们多呀多快乐！
（Oh! You steped on my foot! ）
对不起！没关系。
（Oh! You gave me a surprise! ）
谢谢你！不客气。

Question for Reflection

What would you do and what would you say when you meet with a Chinese friend for the first time?

TEACHING TIP

Students are divided into two teams and they line up in two lines, standing face to face. Each sutdent should find a friend from the other line and greet each other with Chinese way.

ASSESSMENT

Listening

选择图片

Choose the corresponding pictures to the dialogues you have heard twice.

1. A B C

2. A B C

3. A B C

选择答案

Choose the correct answers to the questions you have heard twice.

4. (　　) A Linda有一个姐姐。B Linda爱吃苹果。C Linda是澳大利亚人。

5. (　　) A 没关系。　　　B 我很好。　　　C 不客气。

6. (　　) A 没关系。　　B 我很好。　　C 不客气。

Speaking

听后回答

Listen to the recording carefully then answer the questions.

Prepare some pictures or videos of Confucius and give brief introduction to him. Let students listen twice and answer these questions:

1. 他是谁?
2. 他是哪国人?
3. 他是老师吗?

看图说话

Describe the person in the picture in Chinese.

Reading

选择答案

Choose the correct answers according to the questions in the left column.

1. 她是新同学吗?	□	A 没关系。
2. 认识你很高兴。	□	B 她不是。
3. 对不起!	□	C 我也很高兴。

选词填空

Complete the dialogues with the given words.

A 请　　B 谢谢　　C 哪

4. A:(　　)你!　　B:不客气。
5. A:(　　)喝茶!　　B:谢谢!
6. A:你是(　　)国人? B:我是中国人。

Free Reading

Independent Practice "My Feeling Card" can be used as assessment here. Ask students exchange their cards in pairs and read the information on the cards, then take turns telling the teacher what they read on the cards.

UNIT 3

我们是好朋友

LESSON OBJECTIVES

Language

Students will be able to

- Give a brief introduction for others.
- Use the adverb 真.
- Make questions with 好吗.

Culture

Students will know about

- The situation of international schools in China.

More and more students want to learn Chinese nowadays. Many universities established Chinese language and culture department for the learners from other countries. Meanwhile, many excellent international schools are built for students who are willing to learn Chinese in China rather than their home countries. In these schools, you may meet with the students from many different countries. The students here can obtain a kind of global spirit.

- Chinese people usually hang 福 upside down.

During the traditional Chinese spring festival, people paste the character 福 on the door or on the wall inside. It's very interesting that almost all of the Chinese people hang it upside down. The reason is: 福 means "happiness", 倒 means upside down and 倒 has the same sound with 到 which means "coming; arrived". So 福倒了 is equal to 福到了, which means "happiness is coming".

TARGET VOCABULARY AND SENTENCE STRUCTURE

Vocabulary

朋友　欢迎　您　来　真　漂亮

Notice：欢迎 and 您 appear in level 3 of YCT.

Sentence Structure

(name1)，这是(name2)。
你真漂亮！
喝可乐，好吗？

SUGGESTED ACTIVITIES

Guided Practice

- 字卡游戏 Character Cards Game
  Present the words in two columns, one for monosyllabic words and the other for two-syllable words.
  您　来　真
  朋友　欢迎　漂亮

- 拍词游戏 Fly Swatters

- 师生竞赛 Teacher versus Students

- 画画贴贴 Draw and Paste Workbook
  Draw a picture for your best friend. Cut the Chinese characters and paste them in the right order under the picture and read the phrase.

> **TEACHING TIP**
> Lead students to read the phrase in the right order: 我的好朋友. Then lead them to say this sentence:我的好朋友是（name）.

- 连一连 Match Workbook
  Match the sentences with the correct pictures. The teacher should help students make the right choices.

- 观察与判断 Observe and Judge Workbook
  Choose the correct description for the persons depicted.

> **TEACHING TIP**
> The teacher explains the meaning of the sentences and reminds students observe the main characteristic of each person in the picture. The teacher can also encourage students to find the information about Yao Ming and Fan Bingbing on the internet.

- 来和去 Come and Go Workbook
  Choose the Chinese characters 来 or 去, pasting them in the proper positions. Explain that 来 and 去 convey meaning about movement in different directions just like "come and go" in English, then lead students in finishing the practice in

the workbook.

TEACHING TIP
Give some orders using 来 and 去,asking students follow the orders.

- 写写说说 Let's Trace and Say Workbook
  Prepare some flashcards to present the stroke order of 来, then ask students to trace and read the character. The teacher can also remind students to notice the 福 which hangs upside down in the picture.

- 听听连连 Listen and Match Workbook
  Listen to your teacher, then match the right pictures to the right sentences.
  Read these sentences twice for students:
  1. 欢迎你来我们家。
  2. 你真漂亮!
  3. 我们是好朋友。
  4. 我们喝牛奶,好吗?

- 朋友聚会 Party Time Workbook
  Observe the picture carefully and read the dialogues with your teacher's help. Choose your lucky number from your teacher's number box.
  The students who get 2 or a multiple of 2 will get the chance to invite 2 classmates to practice the dialogue in Chinese before the class.
  Lead students in reading the dialogues and make sure students understand.
  Prepare a number box. Let each student choose a number from the box in several times (10 students at a time). The lucky students who get 2, 4, 6 or 8 will get a chance to present.

TEACHING TIP
The teacher reminds students to do a survey of the things appear in the picture, such as foods, drinks and animal shaped headwear. It's a good chance to review some words learned previously.

Independent Practice

- 讨论 Free Talking
  Divide the class into groups (5-6 students in each group). Give them the main topic in Chinese—朋友, and let them talk about it freely. Then have each group should sum up and present their own opinion, beginning with "朋友means……".

TEACHING TIP
Join the groups in turn, listen carefully and give guidance when needed.

- 字—词—句 Characters—words—sentences

- 接球问答 Get the Ball and Answer My Question
  Ask a question with 好吗. For example:
  我们学汉语，好吗？
  The student who gets the ball should say 好的.
  If he/she answers the questions in Chinese correctly and quickly, he/she will earn the chance to throw the ball and ask others a question with 好吗.

- 耳语 Whispers
  The teacher whispers to the first student of each line:
  你的个子真高！/她的头发真长！/你真漂亮！/米饭真好吃！/牛奶真好喝！

- 介绍新朋友 Introduce a New Friend
  Divide the class into some small groups (3 students in each group). Have everyone try to take the role of a third party and introduce the other two students to each other.

TEACHING TIP
The teacher should make sure that students could read the sentences correctly before this activity.

- 我的故事书 My Story Book
  Ask students to write a story book titled 我的好朋友, encouraging them to compose freely and try to draw some illustrations.

- 课本剧表演 Perform A Script
  Put three students in one group. Act out the script. After practicing, perform in turns and choose the best team.

- 唱一唱 Let's Sing Workbook
  Teachers should encourage students to replace the names with their real names.

♪♫ 我们是好朋友♪♫

这是Tom，这是Linda。
我们是好朋友。
这是和子，这是心爱。
我们是好朋友。
好朋友，好朋友，
欢迎你来我家。
好朋友，好朋友，
我们是好朋友。

Question for Reflection

Why do the Chinese people usually hang the character 福 upside down?

TEACHING TIP

The students who can answer this question most quickly and correctly can get a gift from the teacher (a red card written with 福).

ASSESSMENT

Listening

选择图片

Choose the pictures corresponding to the dialogues you have heard twice.

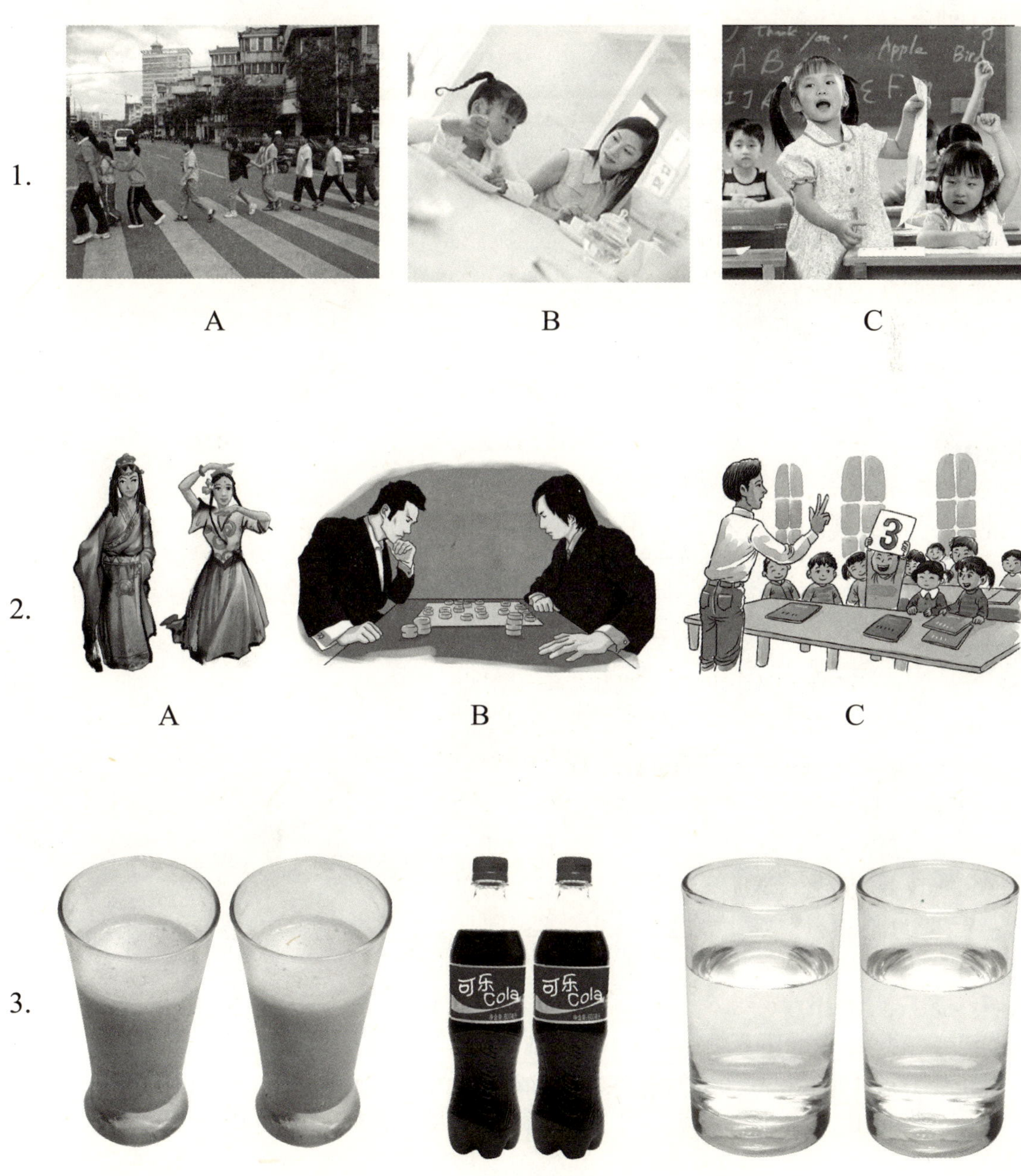

选择答案

Choose the correct answers to the questions you have heard twice.

4. (　　)　A 你好！　B 欢迎你！　C 真漂亮！
5. (　　)　A 他们是好朋友。　B 他们在贝贝家。　C 他们是小学生。
6. (　　)　A 好的。　B 欢迎来我家。　C 是的。

Speaking

听后回答

Read some sentences to introduce a good friend from China. Then ask students to answer the questions.

1. 老师的好朋友叫什么名字？
2. 老师的好朋友是哪国人？
3. 老师的好朋友在哪儿？

Answer the questions that the teacher asked.

4. 你的好朋友是谁？
5. 你的好朋友是哪国人？
6. 你的好朋友今年几岁了？

Reading

选择答案

Choose the correct responses to the sentences in the left column.

1. 你真漂亮！　☐　A 她是我的好朋友！
2. 李心爱是谁？　☐　B 真好喝！
3. 可乐好喝吗？　☐　C 你也很漂亮。

选词填空

Fill in the blanks with the given words.

A 真　　B 好吗　　C 来

4. A：欢迎你（　　）中国！　　B：谢谢！
5. A：周六我们去长城，（　　）？　B：好的。
6. A：你的眼睛（　　）大！　　B：是吗？

Free Reading

Independent Practice "My Story Book" can be used as a rubric for assessment here. Ask students to exchange their storybooks in pairs and retell the stories as possible as they can.

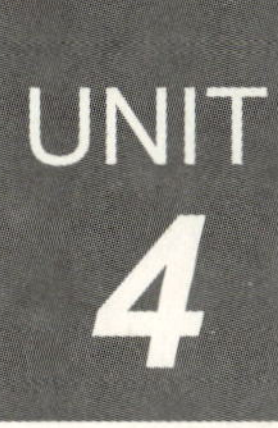

这是谁的房间

LESSON OBJECTIVES

Language

Students will be able to

- Express the existence of something.
- Use the verb有.
- Use the orientation words 里面,上边.

Culture

Students will know about

- Four treasures of study in China.
  In ancient China, the four treasures were important to the students, writers and scholars. They are still a kind of special representative for Chinese culture nowadays.
  笔 brush　　墨 ink stick
  纸 paper　　砚 ink stone

- How to use a Chinese brush.

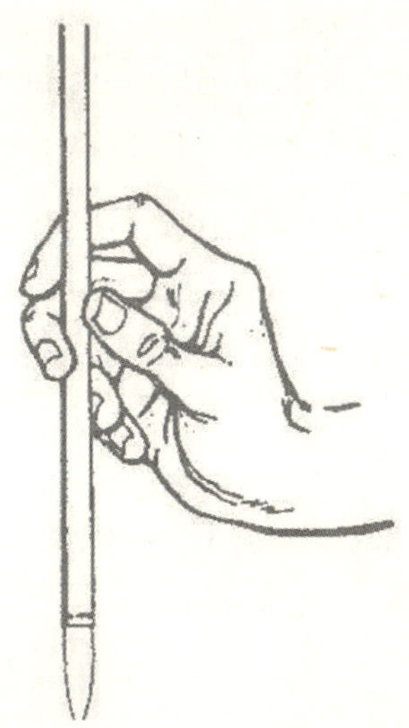

One should hold a brush with five fingers in the way that the picture shows.
Step 1: Hold the brush inside your hand with the first quarter of the thumb and put your forefinger outside the brush. In this way you can grab the brush with these two fingers.
Step 2: Use your middle finger to hold the brush more tightly.
Step 3: Use the ring and little finger to support the pen from the other side.
Step 4: Keep your wrist parallel to the desk, and the pen perpendicular to the paper.
Step 5: Now try to write 一,二,三 with the brush, with ink or water.

TEACHING TIP

The teacher could show this himself/herself or prepare a video to present how to hold a Chinese brush. Then help students to practice with a Chinese brush if possible.

TARGET VOCABULARY AND SENTENCE STRUCTURE

Vocabulary

房间 里面 上边 桌子 椅子
床 书包 铅笔 茶

Sentence Structure

这个房间里有(Noun)。
桌子上边有(Noun)。
书包里面有(Noun)。

SUGGESTED ACTIVITIES

Guided Practice

- 字卡游戏 Character Cards Game
  Present the words in two columns, one for monosyllabic words and the other for two-syllable words.
  床 茶
  房间 里面 上边 桌子 椅子 书包 铅笔

- 拍词游戏 Fly Swatters

- 快速反应 Respond Quickly
  Point to the pictures on the textbook or actual objects and ask:
  (学生1的名字)，这是什么？
  The student should answer the question quickly:
  这是书包。

Then the student continues to ask the next student with the question 这是什么, pointing to another picture or object.

TEACHING TIP
This is a class activity. Students should ask and answer quickly. The one who cannot answer the question in five seconds will be "out". The teacher takes the role of the time counter.

- 画画说说 Draw and Say **Workbook**
  Draw a picture of your room then talk about it with your partner. Lead students to talk about the picture with the sentences employing 有.

- 找不同 Find the Differences **Workbook**
  Find the differences between the pictures and talk about them with your partner, using sentences employing 有.
  Lead students in finding the differences and try to describe them in Chinese.

- 观察与判断 Observe and Judge **Workbook**
  Choose rooms suited for different persons. Then choose your favorite room and describe it.

TEACHING TIP
Divide the class in several groups then lead them in talking about the topic.

- 写写说说 Let's Trace and Say **Workbook**
  Prepare some flashcards to present the correct stroke order for 有, then ask students to trace and read the character.
  You can also provide some additional words for these stationery appearing in the picture (铅笔盒,尺子,橡皮) if students want to know how to say them in Chinese.

- 听听连连 Listen and Match **Workbook**
  Match the pictures to the correct sentences when your teacher read the sentences twice.
  Read these sentences twice:
  1. 学校里有老师和同学。
  2. 这个房间里有桌子、椅子和床。

3. 书包里有很多书。
4. 商场里有很多好吃的。

- 布置房间 Decorate A Room
  Tom's mother bought some new furniture for him and Tom really wants to change the style of his room. Please give him some suggestions. Paste the new things into the picture then try to describe the new design in Chinese.

> **TEACHING TIP**
> Provide some additional words such as 沙发 and 花. Find some volunteers to describe the picture before the class.

Independent Practice

- 讨论 Free Talking
  Divide the class into some groups (5-6 students in each group). Give them the main topic:Tom 的房间, and let them talk about it freely.

- 字—词—句 Characters—words—sentences
  The teacher prepares some character cards. Divide the class in groups, each group including 5 at least. Everyone gets a character card and should find the others to assemble words and sentences quickly. The group which forms most words and sentences will be the winner. The winner should present the words and sentences by standing in a row while holding the cards in the correct order. Other students read the sentences aloud and check if they are correct or not.

- 接球问答 Get the Ball and Answer My Question
  Ask a question employing 有. For example:
  书包里面有什么？
  The student who gets the ball should say 书包里面有铅笔. If he/she answers the questions in Chinese correctly and quickly, he/she will earn the chance to throw the ball and ask another student a question with 有.

- 耳语 Whispers
  Whisper to the first student in each line:
  我的房间里有桌子。
  桌子上边有书包。
  书包里面有苹果。
  椅子上有一只猫。

- 我的房间 My Room
  Divide the class into small groups (3 students in each group). Everyone should prepare a real picture of his/her room. Describe the rooms in Chinese in the group.

- 奇妙的书法 Miracle Calligraphy
  Ask students to find some Chinese calligraphy works from journals or internet, then present them before the class.

- 唱一唱 Let's Sing Workbook

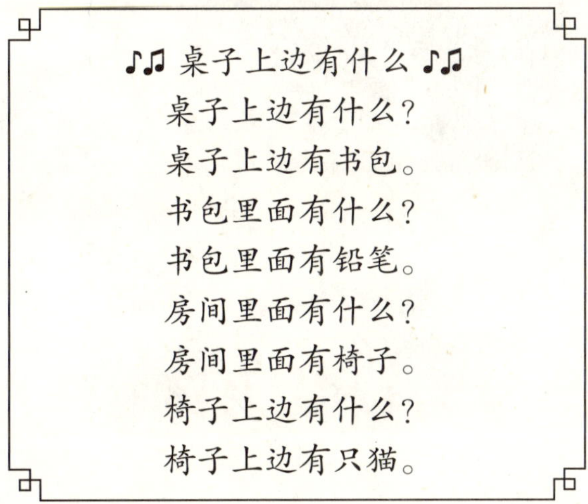

TEACHING TIP
Suggest students to sing this song as quickly as possible.

Question for Reflection
What's the secret for using a Chinese brush?

TEACHING TIP
Find some volunteers to show how to use a Chinese brush. The one who can use it very well can get a gift from the teacher (a real Chinese brush).

ASSESSMENT

Listening

选择图片

Choose the pictures corresponding to the sentences you have heard twice.

A

B

C

1. □
2. □
3. □

选择答案

Choose the correct answers to the questions you have heard twice.

4. ( ) A 很大。B 贝贝的。 C 很好吃。
5. ( ) A 有。 B 是。 C 不是。
6. ( ) A 好的。B 真漂亮! C 有。

Speaking

听后回答

Listen to the teacher carefully then answer the questions.

The teacher provides a picture of a room and reads some sentences to introduce the room. Then ask students to answer the questions.

1. 这是谁的房间?
2. 这个房间里有什么?
3. 你喜欢这个房间吗?

看图说话

Describe the things appearing in the pictures in Chinese.

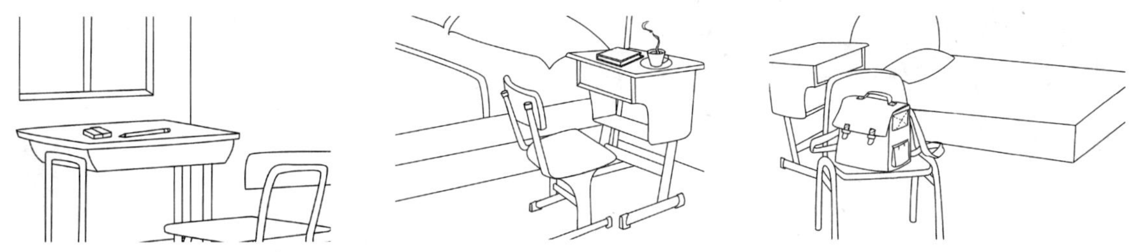

Reading

选择答案

Choose the correct answers to the questions in the left column.

1. 这是 Tom 的房间吗？ ☐ A 有桌子、椅子和床。
2. 你的房间里有什么？ ☐ B 有。
3. 书包里面有铅笔吗？ ☐ C 是。

选词填空

Complete the dialogues with the given words.

A 有　　B 里面　　C 上边

4. A：Tom 的房间里面（　　）桌子吗？ B：（　　）！
5. A：铅笔在哪儿？ B：在书包（　　）。
6. A：书包在哪儿？ B：在椅子（　　）。

Free Reading

Draw a picture according to the description.

这个房间很大。房间里有桌子、椅子和床。桌子上有书和铅笔。我坐在椅子上看书。

UNIT 5

你会不会画画儿

LESSON OBJECTIVES

Language

Students will be able to

- Talk about hobbies.
- Use 会不会 to give questions.
- Use 呢 to give questions.

Culture

Students will know about

- Traditional Chinese Painting.

  Chinese paintings are created by brush drawings in black ink and natural colors on *Xuanzhi*. Traditional Chinese painting topics include figure painting, landscape painting and flower and-bird painting. Compared with western painting, the main characteristics of Chinese painting strives less for realism, but instead tries to display the inner world of the artist – no obvious light and shadows are depicted on the paper because of the absence of a light source; white space is maintained for "implicit beauty".

（唐）周昉《簪花仕女图》

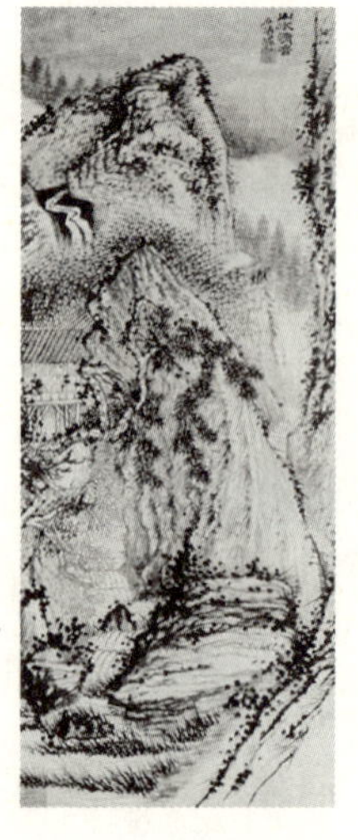

（清）石涛《山水清音图》

李苦禅《双栖图》

Show students some pictures of real mountains or plants, giving them an opportunity to compare the pictures and the Chinese painting. It will help them in their understanding the characteristics of Chinese painting.

- The hobbies of Chinese children.
  Nowadays, Chinese parents want to give more opportunities to their children to learn more about pursuits such as painting, singing, dancing. Children are encouraged to join extracurricular courses in English, science or sports. It's a common situation for a Chinese teenager to have three or four additional classes on the weekend.

TARGET VOCABULARY AND SENTENCE STRUCTURE

Vocabulary

会	说	汉语	学习	两
呢	画	中国画	只	

Sentence Structure

你会不会(Verb+Noun)?
我学习汉语(period)了。
你呢?

SUGGESTED ACTIVITIES

Guided Practice

- 字卡游戏 Character Cards Game
  Present the words in three columns: monosyllabic words, two-syllable words and three-syllable words.
  会 说 两 呢 画
  汉语 学习 中国画

- 师生竞赛 Teacher versus Students

- 我会画 I Can Draw **Workbook**
  Read the following sentences, then draw a picture according to the given descriptions.

  Lead students in reading these sentences:
  我会画画儿。我画了两只鸟。
  我会画画儿。我画了一只狗。
  我会画画儿。我画了一个人。

- 听听连连 Listen and Match **Workbook**
  Listen to your teacher and match the people with the phrases that you have heard.

  Read the sentences twice:
  Tom 会说汉语。Linda 也会说汉语。
  贝贝会画画儿。李心爱也会画画儿。

- 观察与判断 Observe and Judge **Workbook**
  Find traditional Chinese paintings in the pictures.

> **TEACHING TIP**
> The teacher introduces the traditional Chinese paintings and assists students in identifying them.
> It will be helpful if the teacher provides some pictures of traditional Chinese paintings.

- 写写说说 Let's Trace and Say **Workbook**
  Practice in pairs.Make questions with 会不会 according to the pictures and ask your partner to answer the questions.
  The teacher should prepare flashcards to present the structure and stroke order of 会. Then encourage students to write and read it.

> **TEACHING TIP**
> The teacher asks students to practice in pairs, providing some suggestions as to the key elements in the pictures if needed.

- 调查 Do A Survey **Workbook**
  Interview three or four classmates to make sure of some information. Then write down their names and circle their answers.

- “二”和“两” Workbook

  Read the phrases aloud and try to find the different usages of 二 and 两.

  The teacher explains the different usages of 二 and 两：

  二 is used for counting; 两 has to be used with a measure word following. For example:

  一二三四五

  第一 第二 第三

  两个人 两只鸟 两个朋友

Independent Practice

- 西蒙说 Simon Says

  Divide the class in some groups. Play this game with these verbs:

  画画　学习　说汉语　吃饭　喝水

- 字—词—句 Characters—words—sentences

- 耳语 Whispers

  The teacher whispers to the first student in each line:

  你会不会画画儿？

  我会说汉语。你呢？

  我学习汉语两年了。

  我很喜欢中国画。

- 我的故事书 My Story Book

  Make a story book which focuses on your hobbies.You can use some Chinese words or sentences in your book, such as:

  喜欢 不喜欢 会 不会

  画画儿 说汉语 唱歌

- 课本剧表演 Perform A Script

  Perform the script in pairs. After practicing, perform in turn and choose the best team.

- 唱一唱 Let’s Sing Workbook

  Ask students to sing this song in pairs and in two groups.

♪♫ 你会不会说汉语♪♫

你好吗？你好吗？
你会不会说汉语？
我会说，我会说，
我们来说汉语吧！
你好吗？你好吗？
你会不会画画儿？
我会画，我会画，
我们来画中国画儿。
你好吗？你好吗？
你会不会唱歌啊？
我会唱，我会唱，
我们来唱汉语歌。

Question for Reflection

What are the main differences of traditional Chinese painting and western painting?

TEACHING TIP

The teacher provides more pictures of traditional Chinese paintings and western paintings. Encourage students to find the difference and describe the features of Chinese painting in their eyes. Then the teacher gives a summary with some common features of traditional Chinese painting and western painting.

ASSESSMENT

Listening

选择图片

Choose the pictures corresponding to the sentences you have heard twice.

A

B

C

1. □
2. □
3. □

选择答案

Choose the correct answers to the questions you have heard wice.

4. (　　) A 有。　B 是。　C 会。
5. (　　) A 很好。　B 我也是。　C 你好。
6. (　　) A 漂亮。　B 会。　C 不会。

Speaking

听后回答

Listen to the recording carefully, then answer the questions.

Prepare a recording which introduces the experiences of a Chinese language learner. Students listen twice then answer these questions:

1. 他会不会说汉语？　2. 他学习汉语几年了？　3. 他会不会画画儿？

看图说话

Describe the picture in Chinese.

Reading

选择答案

Choose the correct answers to the questions in the left column.

1. 她会不会说汉语? □ A 两年了。
2. 这是中国画吗? □ B 会。
3. 你学汉语几年了? □ C 是。

选词填空

Complete the dialogues with the given words.

A 不　　B 两　　C 呢

4. A：你会（　　）会画中国画儿?　　B：我会。
5. A：我来中国（　　）年了。　　B：我来中国三年了。
6. A：我学习汉语一年了，你（　　）?　B：我学习汉语五年了。

Free Reading

Independent Practice "My Story Book" can be used as assessment here. Ask students to exchange their story books in pairs and read the information on the books. Then try to retell the stories in Chinese.

UNIT 6

打电话

LESSON OBJECTIVES

Language

Students will be able to

- Understand and use some common words for telephone calls in Chinese.
- Ask for others' opinions or suggestions with 怎么样.

Culture

Students will know about

- Some useful expressions for telephone calls in Chinese.
  To greet each other: 喂？（Hello?）
  To make a self-introduction: 你好！我是Tom。（Hello! I am Tom.）
  To confirm the identity of a caller: 请问，是Linda吗？（Excuse me, is that Linda?）
  To express agreement: 嗯。（Hmm.）
  To ask others to wait for a moment: 请等一下。（Hold on, please.）
  Say goodbye: 好的，再见！（Ok, goodbye!）

- Some country codes.
  美国 U.S.A. 001
  中国 China 0086
  加拿大 Canada 001
  澳大利亚 Australia 0061
  韩国 Korea 0082
  日本 Japan 0081

TEACHING TIP
The teacher can provide more country codes if the students want to know more. Students can also learn some country names in Chinese according to their interests.

TARGET VOCABULARY AND SENTENCE STRUCTURE

Vocabulary

打电话　　喂　　动物园　　熊猫

Notice: 喂 and 动物园 appear in level 3 of YCT.

Sentence Structure

喂……

怎么样?

SUGGESTED ACTIVITIES

Guided Practice

- Greeting Each Other on the Line

  Give a call to a student:

  喂?（学生1的名字），你好!

  The student should continue to say this sentence to his/her classmates. If one can't respond in time, he/she should sing a song or tell a story in Chinese.

- 拍词游戏 Fly Swatters

- 快速反应 Respond Quickly

  Give an order in this format:

  (学生1的名字), give a call to (学生2的名字)，please.

  Then the first student should "call" their specified contact.

  They will have a conversation like this:

  学生1：喂? 你好! 是（学生2的名字）吗?

  学生2：我是（学生2的名字）。你是谁?

  学生1：我是（学生1的名字）。

  The one who cannot respond within 5 seconds will be "out".

- 听听写写 Listen and Write **Workbook**

  Listen to your teacher carefully then write down the telephone numbers which you hear. Find the correct Chinese characters to record these numbers.

  Read the telephone numbers for twice.
  Tom的电话是50026097。
  Linda 的电话是39006280。
  贝贝的电话是 50026628。
  李心爱的电话是39002521。
  和子的电话是62620033。

- 紧急求助电话 Urgent Telephone Numbers **Workbook**

  Read these numbers in Chinese and try to remember them.

  > **TEACHING TIP**
  > Explain emergency situations and lead students in reading these numbers in Chinese.

- 写写说说 Let's Trace and Say **Workbook**

  Prepare some flashcards to present the stroke order of "电". Then ask students to trade and read this character.

- 调查 A Survey of Country Codes **Workbook**

- 说一说 Let's Talk **Workbook**

  Paul is a panda who lives in America and Jingjing is his friend who lives in Beijing, China. They talked with each other today. Please complete their dialogue with the given words. Then practice this dialogue with your partner.

  > **TEACHING TIP**
  > Lead students in practicing the dialogue in pairs. Then divide the class in 2 groups and practice it again.

- 怎么样? How About It?

  Prepare some cards with words in four categories. These words are recommended:
  时间词：星期一 星期二 星期三 星期四 星期五 星期六 星期天 今天 明天 昨天
  处所词：学校 商店 动物园 家 房间
  人名：（几个学生的真实名字）

助词：的
Ask 4 volunteers to choose one card from each type. Have them show the cards to the class, asking their classmates to form a sentence with these words. He who forms a correct sentence will get the chance to choose the word cards and continue the game. For example:
星期六我们去（学生1的名字）家怎么样?

Independent Practice

- 讨论 Free Talking
  Divide the class into groups (5-6 students in each group), asking them to record the telephone numbers of everyone in the group.

- 接球问答 Get the Ball and Answer My Question
  Ask a question with 怎么样. For example:
  今天我们去商店怎么样?
  The student who gets the ball should say 好的. If he/she answers the questions in Chinese correctly and quickly, he/she will earn the chance to throw the ball and ask others question with 怎么样.

- 耳语 Whispers
  Whisper to the first student in each line:
  喂？你好！我是王老师。
  明天我们去动物园怎么样?
  我的电话是12345678。

- 我们的同学录 Classmate Contact Book
  Divide the class into small groups. Each group should interview some students from other classes and record their names and telephone numbers if possible.

- 约定 Make An Appointment
  Ask students to call each other in pairs after class and make an appointment for the weekend.

TEACHING TIP
Students should report how they spend the weekend together as planned next week.

- 越洋电话 Overseas Call
  Students are required to call each other in pairs as two friends from different

countries, using the correct country codes that the teacher provides.

- 唱一唱 Let's Sing **Workbook**
  Ask students to sing this song in pairs and in two groups.

♪♫ 打电话 ♪♫

喂？喂？喂？你是 Tom吗？
我是 Tom，你好，你好！
今天我们去动物园，怎么样？怎么样？
好，好，好！我们去动物园！
喂？喂？喂？你是 Linda吗？
我是 Linda，你好，你好！
明天我们去商店，怎么样？怎么样？
对不起，我还要去学校。
喂？喂？喂？你是心爱吗？
我是心爱，你好，你好！
明天我们去学校，怎么样？怎么样？
好，好，好！我们去学校。

TEACHING TIP
Ask students to sing this song in two groups, one group takes the role of A and the other sings as B.

Question for Reflection

How do you ask for feedback or suggestions in Chinese?

TEACHING TIP
Give students some specific situations that need to ask for other's feedback or suggestion. For example:
我们去商店，______？
我们去吃饭，______？
我们画中国画，______？

ASSESSMENT

Listening

选择图片

Choose the pictures corresponding to the sentences you have heard twice.

A

Liu Yueyan
Editor
Chinese Publications International
36, Wang Fu Jing Str. Beijing,
100710, China
Tel: (010)65258899-214
Mobile: 13811276262
Fax: (010)65140248
E-mail: liuyueyan@cp.com.cn

B

C

1. □
2. □
3. □

选择答案

Choose the correct answers to the questions you have heard twice.

4. (　　) A 我和李心爱。 B 我认识李心爱。 C 我是李心爱。
5. (　　) A 有。 B 好的。 C 是。
6. (　　) A 我们明天见。 B 我们星期六见。 C 我们学校见。

Speaking

听后回答

Listen to the recording carefully then answer the questions.

Prepare a recording of two students who are making an appointment on the phone. Ask students to listen and answer these questions in turns.

1. 他们是谁?
2. 他们去哪儿?
3. 他们在哪儿见?

看图说话

Describe the animal in the picture in Chinese.

Reading

选择答案

Choose the correct response to the sentences in the left column.

1. 喂？你是和子吗?	☐	A 动物园。
2. 这个房间怎么样?	☐	B 是。
3. 去哪儿看熊猫?	☐	C 很漂亮。

选词填空

Complete the dialogues with the given words.

A 电话　B 怎么样　C 喂

4. A：（　　）？你好！我是王小月。B：你好！
5. A：我们去Linda家（　　）？　B：好的。
6. A：贝贝的（　　）呢?　B：我知道！50026628。

Free Reading

Independent Practice "Classmate Contact Book" can be used as assessment here. Ask students to exchange their reports in pairs and read the information on the cards. Then tell the teacher the telephone numbers of at least 2 classmates.

UNIT 7

贝贝的一天

LESSON OBJECTIVES

Language

Students will be able to

- Express the exact time.
- Use the time and location adverbially.

Culture

Students will understand

- Scheduling in Chinese schools.
  Chinese pupils usually go to school before 8:00 in the morning, with some international schools beginning at 8:30 or 9:00. Class ends at 4:10 in the afternoon, when some of the pupils go to additional classes inside or outside of school. Others return home and finish their homework.

- 时差 Time Difference
  时差 means time difference, which refers to the difference in local time between two areas. For example, China is the east eight region (GMT +8), the eastern United States is west five region (GMT –5). There are 13 hours between Beijing and New York and the former is earlier. It also refers to jet lag, the fatigue and sleep disturbance resulting from disruption of the body's normal circadian rhythm as a result of jet travel.

国名	城市	与北京时差	国名	城市	与北京时差
美国	旧金山	–16	匈牙利	布达佩斯	–7
墨西哥	墨西哥城	–15	罗马尼亚	布加勒斯特	–6
美国	纽约	–13	埃及	开罗	–6
巴拿马	巴拿马城	–13	俄罗斯	莫斯科	–5

加拿大	蒙特利亚	–13	印度	新德里	–2.30
古巴	哈瓦那	–13	斯里兰卡	科伦城	–2.30
法国	巴黎	–8	新加坡	新加坡	–0.30
英国	伦敦	–8	印尼	雅加达	–0.30
意大利	罗马	–7	马来西亚	吉隆坡	–0.30
东德	柏林	–7	菲律宾	马尼拉	–0.30
波兰	华沙	–7	朝鲜	平壤	+1
瑞士	日内瓦	–7	日本	东京	+1
捷克	布拉格	–7	澳大利亚	悉尼	+2

TARGET VOCABULARY AND SENTENCE STRUCTURE

Vocabulary

起床　吧　分钟　早上　包子
香蕉　晚上　睡觉　玩

Sentence Structure

七点四十分。
(people)(time)(action)。
(people)在(place) (action)。

SUGGESTED ACTIVITIES

Guided Practice

- 字卡游戏 Character Cards Game

- 拍词游戏 Fly Swatters

- 猜一猜 Guess the Words
  Ask a volunteer to act out the meaning of the words, while other students try to guess the Chinese words and say the words aloud.
  起床 睡觉 吃饭 喝水 玩

- 认识时间 Figure the Time **Workbook**
  Figure the time out and write it down in the blanks provided.

> **TEACHING TIP**
> Assist students in figuring out the exact time according to the pictures. Encourage them to say the time in Chinese aloud.

- 听听连连 Listen and Match **Workbook**
  Listen to your teacher, then match the time with the situation that you heard.

  Read these sentences twice.
  我早上七点起床。
  我七点四十去学校。
  十二点，我和同学们在学校吃饭。
  五点，我在家学习中国画。
  晚上九点，我睡觉。
  Lead students in describing the pictures with the sentences above.

> **TEACHING TIP**
> Lead students notice that the position of the subjects of these sentences is flexible. 我早上七点起床 and 早上七点我起床 are both correct. The time information was emphasized somehow in the latter pattern.

- 写写说说 Let's Trace and Say **Workbook**
  Prepare some flashcards to present the structure and the stroke order of 天, then encourage students to write and read it.

- 观察与判断 Observe and Judge **Workbook**
  Choose the correct description for the pictures.
  Ask students to talk about the right descriptions of the cases with their partners.

- 今天你做什么了 What Did You Do Today

Ask a student with this sentence:
今天我看书了。（学生1的名字），你呢？
The student should answer this question in Chinese, then, he/she can ask another student this sentence:
今天我学习汉语了。（学生2的名字），你呢？
This dialogue will continue till someone can't answer. Instead of answering, he/she should sing a Chinese song or tell a short story in Chinese.

Independent Practice

- 西蒙说 Simon Says
  The teacher asks students to stand in a big circle and play this game. The one whose role is Simon should use these verbs when he/she gives orders to others.
  吃饭　喝水　睡觉　起床　玩　学习　画画

- 字—词—句 Characters—Words—Sentences

- 耳语 Whispers
  Whisper to the first student in each line:
  我早上六点起床。
  我在家里喝牛奶。
  她晚上九点睡觉。
  我们在学校学习汉语。

- 我的日程 My Schedule Workbook
  Students are to talk about their daily life in pairs and pay special attention to the usages of the adverbial time phrase in Chinese.

- 美好的一天 A Nice Day
  Make a story book telling the story of a nice day, expressing what happened to you through pictures indicators written in Chinese.

- 课本剧表演 Perform A Script
  Put three students in one group. After practicing the script, perform in turn and choose the best team.

- 唱一唱 Let's Sing Workbook
  Practice this song in pairs. Then divide the whole class into two groups and practice it. Ask students to clap their hands with correct rhythm while singing.

♪♫ 我的一天 ♪♫

早上七点我起床，我起床。（拍手）
七点十分吃早饭，吃早饭。（拍手）
七点四十去学校，去学校，去学校。
七点四十，我们去学校。（拍手）
学习汉语和画画儿，我喜欢。（拍手）
晚上九点我睡觉，我睡觉。（拍手）
这是我的一天，我的一天。
一天一天，又一天。（拍手）

Question for Reflection

What are you doing when the pupils begin their first class at 8:00 AM in China? What time is it in your country?

TEACHING TIP

The teacher provides the exact information of time difference before asking students to answer this question.

ASSESSMENT

Listening

选择图片

Choose the pictures corresponding to the dialogues you have heard twice.

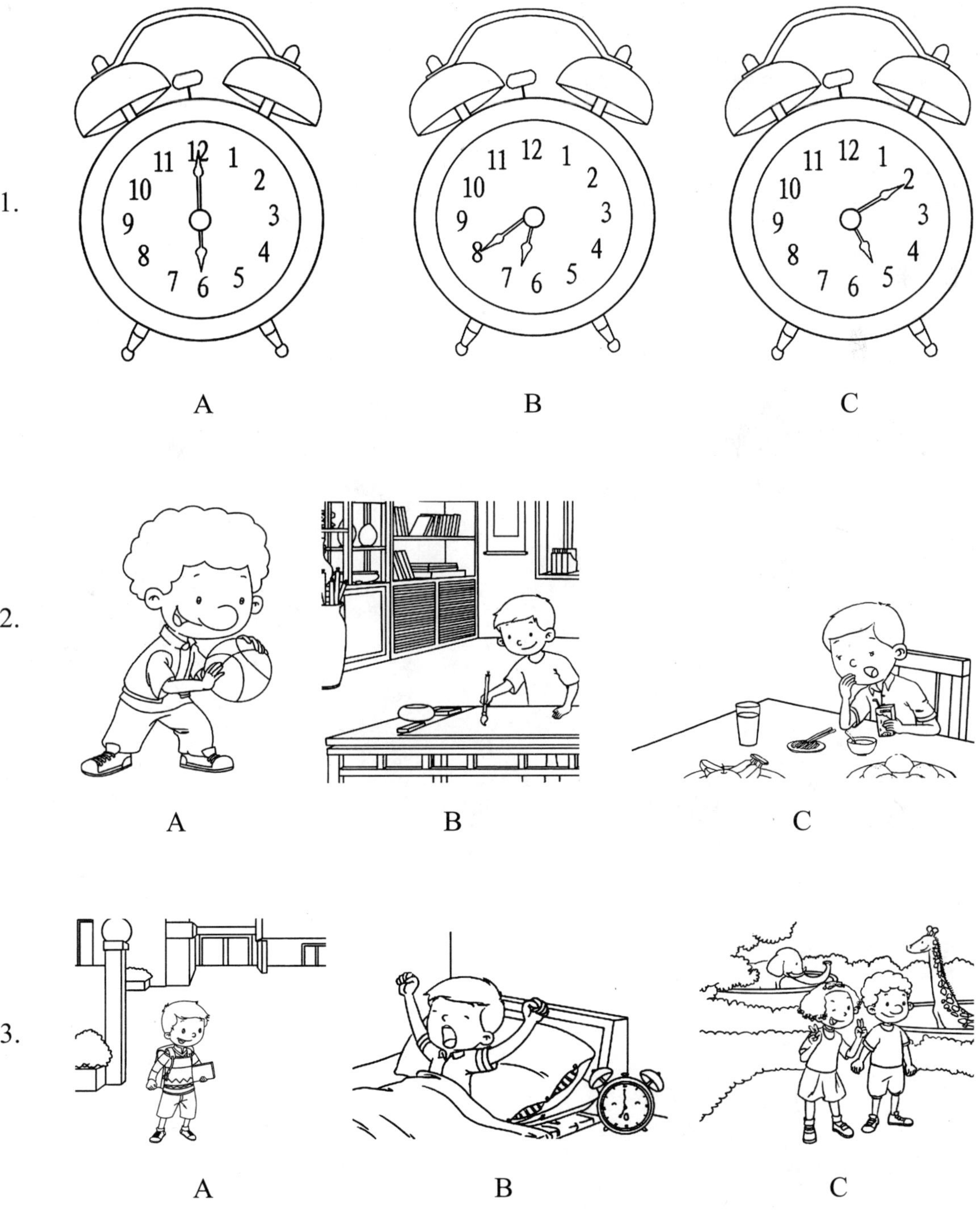

选择答案

Choose the correct response to the sentences you have heard twice.

4. (　　) A 吃吧。　　B 好的。　　C 去学校吧。
5. (　　) A 五点。　　B 很喜欢。　　C 在家。
6. (　　) A 我去学校。　　B 我吃了包子。　　C 我会说汉语。

Speaking

听后回答

Listen to your teacher carefully, then answer the questions.

Read your own schedule twice. Then ask students these questions in turn.

1. 老师早上几点起床？
2. 老师在哪儿吃饭？
3. 老师几点来学校？

讲故事

Recount the story presented in the pictures.

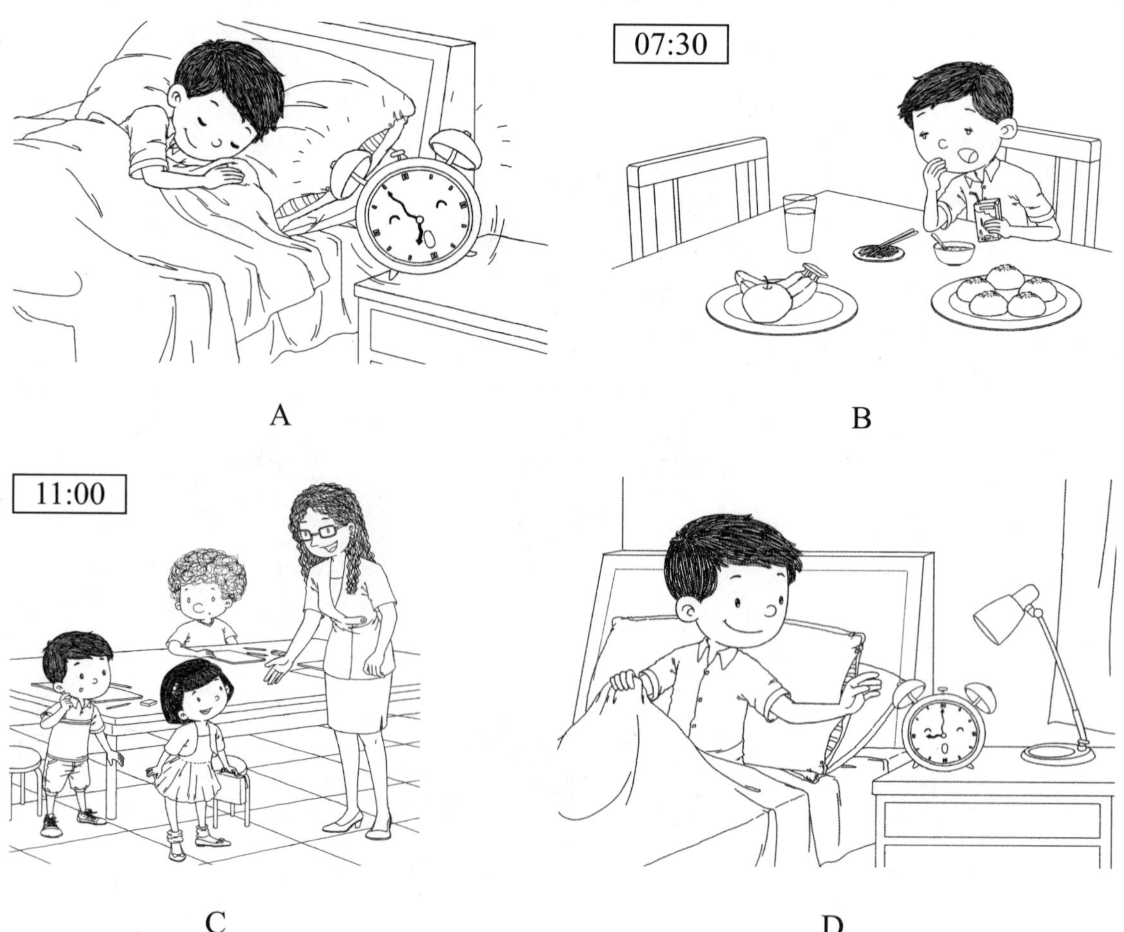

A　B　C　D

Reading

选择答案

Choose the correct answers to the questions in the left column.

1. 你几点去学校？ □ A 晚上九点三十分。
2. 你在哪儿学汉语？ □ B 早上八点。
3. 你几点睡觉？ □ C 在学校。

选词填空

Complete the dialogues with the given words.

A 分　　B 在　　C 了

4. A：你早上吃（　　）什么？ B：包子和牛奶。
5. A：你几点起床？ B：七点二十（　　）。
6. A：你在哪儿学中国画儿？ B：（　　）学校。

Free Reading

Independent Practice "A Nice Day" can be used as a rubric assessment here. Ask students to exchange their story books in pairs, reading and retelling the stories in Chinese.

UNIT 8

你有哥哥吗

LESSON OBJECTIVES

Language

Students should be able to

- Understand and use 有 to express possession.
- Use 没有 to specify "don't/doesn't have".
- Make questions with有没有 or 有……吗.

Culture

Students will know about

- Big families in ancient China.

  In ancient China, people favored big families. Parents wanted to have more children, especially more sons. The eldest son enjoyed a special position and rights in the family. There is an old saying in China: Brothers are like hands and feet.

- The only child in a Chinese family.
  Nowadays, most families only have one child in China, so parents and grandparents give all of their love to this single child. It has become a social problem gradually, as these children hardly have opportunity to share with others when they are very young. Many Chinese parents have realized this and try to encourage their kids to spend more time with peers.

TARGET VOCABULARY AND SENTENCE STRUCTURE

Vocabulary

帅　　没有　　弟弟　　妹妹

Sentence Structure

我有一个弟弟。
我没有妹妹。
你有……（Noun）吗？/ 你有没有……（Noun）？

SUGGESTED ACTIVITIES

Guided Practice

- 家庭成员 Family Members
  Show some family pictures and provide the cards with the words 爸爸, 妈妈, 哥哥, 姐姐, 弟弟, 妹妹. Describe this family with the sentences:
  我有一个哥哥，我没有姐姐。
  Encourage students to present their own family pictures and describe them in Chinese.

- 我的兄弟姐妹 My Brothers and Sisters Workbook
  Fill in the blanks with real information about your family.
  Lead students in filling in the forms with their true information, then ask them to talk about their reports in pairs.

- 他很帅 He Is Handsome
  Provide some pictures of famous stars that are familiar to students. Then ask students to describe them with the sentences:
  他很帅。/ 他不帅。
  她很漂亮。/ 她不漂亮。
  他很高。/ 他不高。

A

B

C

D

E

Then ask students to designate the most handsome man or most beautiful woman in their mind one by one. For example:
The first student says:
奥巴马很帅，奥普拉很漂亮。
The second student says:
奥巴马不帅，姚明很帅。奥普拉不漂亮，我妈妈很漂亮。
He/she can also express agreement with these sentences:
是的，他很帅。/是的，她很漂亮。

- 快速反应 Respond Quickly
  Divide the class into groups of 5 students. They should ask each other some questions with 有没有 or 有……吗; the person asked should respond quickly. For example:
  你有没有姐姐？/ 你有姐姐吗？
  我有两个姐姐。/ 我没有姐姐。
  你有没有铅笔？/ 你有铅笔吗？
  我有铅笔。/ 我没有铅笔。
  Then ask the groups to give a presentation before the class.

- 听听连连 Listen and Match **Workbook**
  Listen to your teacher and match the persons with the phrases that you hear.
  Read the Chinese sentences twice:
  Tom有一个哥哥。

贝贝没有哥哥姐姐，也没有弟弟妹妹。
Linda有一个姐姐。
李心爱有一个弟弟。
和子有一个妹妹。

- 写写说说 Let's Trace and Say **Workbook**
  Prepare some flashcards to present the stroke order of 有, then ask students to trade and read this character.

- 观察与判断 Observe and Judge **Workbook**
  Find the exact relationships of these children who are brothers and sisters according to the clues that appear in the picture. Then complete the sentences with the stickers.

> **TEACHING TIP**
> Remind students to notice all the details in the picture and helps them to find the correct answers.

- 听听读读 Listen and Read **Workbook**
  Complete the sentences according to the ones you have heard. Then read them aloud.
  Read the Chinese sentences twice:
  你有弟弟吗？有。我的弟弟很帅！
  你有妹妹吗？有。我的妹妹很漂亮！
  你有铅笔吗？有。我的铅笔很多！
  你有书包吗？有。我的书包很大！

- 看图说话 Story Telling **Workbook**
  Tell a story in Chinese according to the picture, using the given words as you can.

> **TEACHING TIP**
> Ask students to read the given words aloud. Then lead students in analyzing the picture carefully and encourage students to speak more in Chinese.

Independent Practice

- 讨论 Free Talking
  Divide the class into groups (5-6 students in each group), asking them to talk freely about their family members in Chinese.

- 接球问答 Get the Ball and Answer My Question
  The teacher asks a question with有没有or 有……吗. For example:
  （学生1的名字），你有没有哥哥？
  The student who gets the ball should say：
  我有一个哥哥。/ 我没有哥哥。
  If he/she answers the questions in Chinese correctly and quickly, he/she will earn the chance to throw the ball and ask others questions with 有没有or 有……吗.
  The teacher should remind students to notice that 有没有 never appears with 吗 in the same sentence.

- 耳语 Whispers
  Whisper to the first student in each line:
  我有一个弟弟。他很帅。
  我有一个妹妹。她很漂亮。
  我没有哥哥。
  你有没有中国朋友？

- 调查 A Survey of Brothers and Sisters Workbook
  Interview your best friends and find out if they have brothers or sisters and if they like their brothers or sisters or not.
  Ask students to bring their reports to the class and give a presentation.
  The last 3 sentences in the Textbook should be changed to the following ones:
  你喜欢你的弟弟吗？/你喜欢你的姐姐吗？/你喜欢你的妹妹吗？

- 我的故事书 My Story Book
  Ask students to make a story book which concerns some interesting experiences with their brothers or sisters.

- 我有…… I Have…
  Ask students to consider about what they have in this stage of life, then make a card to express it with pictures or Chinese sentences if possible.

TEACHING TIP
Encourage students to practice using different adjectives and nouns. For example:
我有一个新书包。/ 我有一个漂亮姐姐。/ 我有三个好朋友。

- 唱一唱 Let's Sing Workbook
  Divide the class in groups. All of the students in the same group stand in a circle

hand in hand. Practice this song while dancing freely.

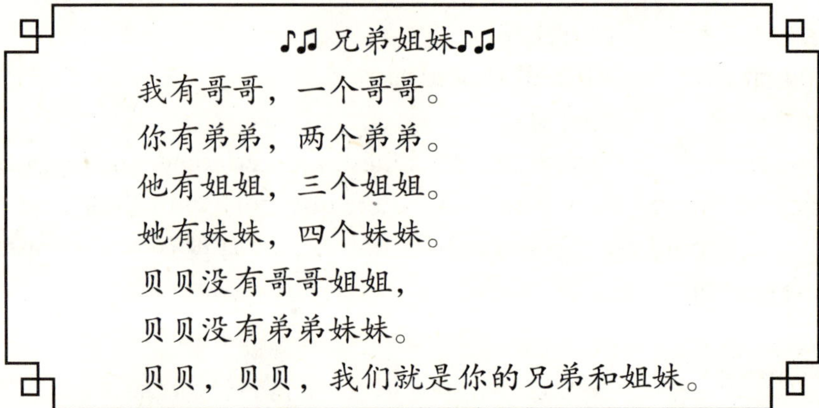

Question for Reflection

Do you have a good time when you stay with your brother or sister? Why?

TEACHING TIP

Encourage students to tell something about their brothers or sisters and also talk about their experiences when they stay with their brothers or sisters.

ASSESSMENT

Listening

选择图片

Choose the pictures corresponding to the dialogues you have heard twice.

选择答案

Choose the correct responses to the sentences you have heard twice.

4. （　　）A 是。　　B 有。　　C 好。
5. （　　）A 五点。　B 五个。　C 有。
6. （　　）A 是。　　B 有。　　C 很帅。

Speaking

听后回答

Listen to your teacher carefully then answer the questions.

Introduce your brothers or sisters twice. For extra material, you can provide some real pictures of them. Then ask students these questions in turn.

1. 老师有没有哥哥姐姐？
2. 老师有没有弟弟妹妹？
3. 他们怎么样？

讲故事

Tell a story about your brothers or sisters.

Encourage students to speak more in Chinese.

Reading

选择答案

Choose the correct answers to the questions in the left column.

1. 你有姐姐吗？　☐　A 三岁。
2. Tom的哥哥帅吗？　☐　B 没有。
3. 你妹妹几岁？　☐　C 帅。

选词填空

Complete the dialogues with the given words.

A 吗　　B 有没有　　C 很

4. A：王贝贝有几个好朋友？B：他的好朋友（　　）多。
5. A：你有弟弟（　　）？　B：没有。
6. A：你（　　）汉语书？　B：有。

Free Reading

Independent Practice "I Have…" can be used as a rubric for assessment here. Ask students to exchange their cards in pairs, reading and retelling their wishes in Chinese.

UNIT 9

这个书包多少钱

LESSON OBJECTIVES

Language

Students will be able to

- Ask prices with 多少钱.
- Declare opinions with 我觉得.
- Get a conclusion with 是……的.

Culture

Students will know about

- Colors in Chinese culture.

  Chinese people love traditionally red. Red is the color of the festivals and almost all of the happy moments in life. Yellow was the royal color in ancient China. The common people had no right to use this color in their lives. It was also considered a refined color which was used in Buddhism. Purple represents auspicious events, and grave and noble style. White is the color of mourning in Chinese traditional culture. It usually represents profound sadness in funerals.

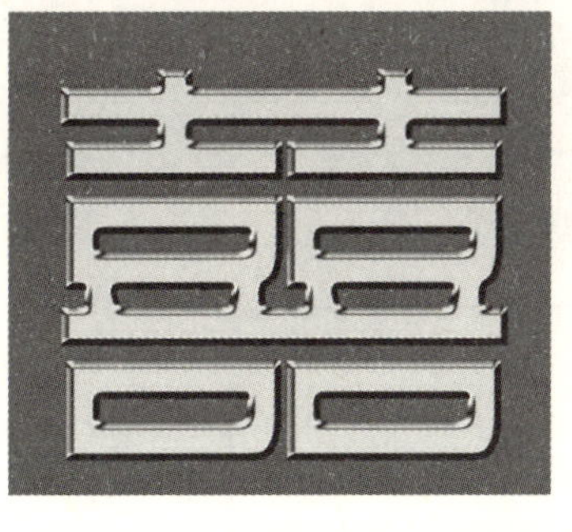

A

B

C

- The comparison of different meanings of the colors in Chinese and English nowadays.

Explain that some traditional meanings of the colors in Chinese have been changed nowadays.
Then compare the different meanings of colors briefly:

Colors	Meanings	
	Chinese	English
Red 红色	*Happiness*	*Happiness(sometimes)*
White 白色	*Sadness (traditionally)* *Purity(sometimes)*	*Purity*
Yellow 黄色	*Royal color(traditionally)* *Common color(nowadays)*	*Timid(sometimes)*
Purple 紫色	*Noble style*	*Noble style*
Black 黑色	*Dark, insidious*	*Dark, insidious*
Green 绿色	*Civilians, commonness(traditionally)* *Environmental protection(nowadays)*	*Rich, naive*

TARGET VOCABULARY AND SENTENCE STRUCTURE

Vocabulary

要 买 书 颜色 红 绿
黄 觉得 多少 钱 块

Sentence Structure

我要买……(goods)
多少钱?
我觉得……(comment or suggestion)
这个书包是绿色的。

SUGGESTED ACTIVITIES

Guided Practice

- 字卡游戏 Character Cards Game

  Present the words in two columns, monosyllabic words and two-syllable words.

  要　买　书　红　绿　黄　钱　块

  颜色　觉得　多少

- 猜一猜 Guess the Colors

  Prepare some fruits or other colorful things. Put them in a big bag and let students guess what color it is before taking it out of the bag. The student who gets the correct answer will continue this game and let others guess.

> **TEACHING TIP**
>
> The teacher can provide other words for colors if needed. For example: 蓝色(blue),白色(white),橙色(orange).

- 多少钱 How Much Is It

  Provide the prices of the things which appeared in activity 2 (Guess the colors), asking two volunteers to take the roles of buyer and seller. They will practice the dialogue below.

  A：你要买什么？
  B：我要买……

  A：你喜欢什么颜色？
  B：我喜欢……

  A：这个怎么样？
  B：多少钱？
  A：……块钱。

- 画一画 Let's Draw **Workbook**

  Draw the pictures according to the given descriptions.

- 说一说 Let's Talk

  Talk about the things in your picture with your partner, using a sentence of the form 是……的.

  Lead students in drawing the things and practice the dialogue in pairs. For example:

  A：苹果是什么颜色的？

B：苹果是红色的。

- 数硬币 Coin Count Workbook
  Count the coins and fill in the blanks.

> **TEACHING TIP**
> Show some real Chinese coins or the pictures of Chinese coins and introduce the Chinese coins of different par values briefly before practicing this.

- 读一读 Let's Read Workbook
  Read the prices on the labels.
  Lead students in reading the prices correctly.

- 购物 Shopping Workbook
  Make a shopping plan.

> **TEACHING TIP**
> Introduce Chinese paper money briefly first (with real Chinese paper money or pictures), then lead students in making their shopping plans.

- 听听连连 Listen and Match Workbook
  Match objects to their correct colors and prices according to what you have heard.
  Read these sentences twice:
  苹果是什么颜色的？苹果是红色的。
  苹果多少钱？十块钱。
  书包是什么颜色的？书包是绿色的。
  书包多少钱？这个书包三十块钱。
  铅笔是什么颜色的？铅笔是黄色的。
  铅笔多少钱？三块钱。

  Prepare some flashcards to present the structure and the stroke order of 买, then encourage students to write and read it.

Independent Practice

- 西蒙说 Simon Says
  Divide the class in some groups, with each one preparing some colored pencils. Then play this game. For example：

One person says:
Simon says: 红色的铅笔
The others should raise the red pencil. Students who respond incorrectly are "out".

- 字—词—句 Characters—Words—Sentences
  These words should be included：
  买　多少　钱　块　颜色　红　绿　黄
  书包　铅笔　书　牛奶　香蕉　包子　米饭

- 耳语 Whispers
  Whisper to the first student in each line:
  我要买书包。
  我要买一个绿色的书包。
  你觉得红色的书包怎么样?
  她的书包是黄色的。

- 我的理财计划 My Budget
  Make a budget assuming you have $1000.

My budget	
Save:	
Shopping: *我要买*	
Share:	

TEACHING TIP
The teacher asks students to hand in their reports within 10–15minutes. Then choose the best budget. The student who designed it will get a small gift from the teacher.

- 色彩调查 A Survey of Color Workbook
  Interview your families and write a report focusing on their favorite colors. Try to describe the result in Chinese.

- 怎么样 How about It Workbook
  Fill in the blanks in the dialogues. Then ask students to talk with each other

according to the text.

- 课本剧表演 Perform A Script
  Act out the script in groups of 3. After practicing, act in turn and choose the best performer.

- 唱一唱 Let's Sing **Workbook**

♪♫ 我要买…… ♪♫

今天星期一，我要买铅笔。
铅笔多少钱？一块一毛一。
多少钱？多少钱？铅笔多少钱？
铅笔的价钱是一块一毛一。
今天星期二，我要买苹果。
苹果多少钱？两块两毛二。
多少钱？多少钱？苹果多少钱？
苹果的价钱是两块两毛二。
今天星期三，我要买书包。
书包多少钱？十块三毛三。
多少钱？多少钱？书包多少钱？
书包的价钱是十块三毛三。

Question for Inflection

What kind of color would you prefer to dress in if you were invited to a Chinese New Year's party?

TEACHING TIP

Show some videos or pictures of Chinese New Year's party. Lead students in finding the suitable colors to dress.

ASSESSMENT

Listening

选择图片

Choose the pictures corresponding to the dialogues you have heard twice.

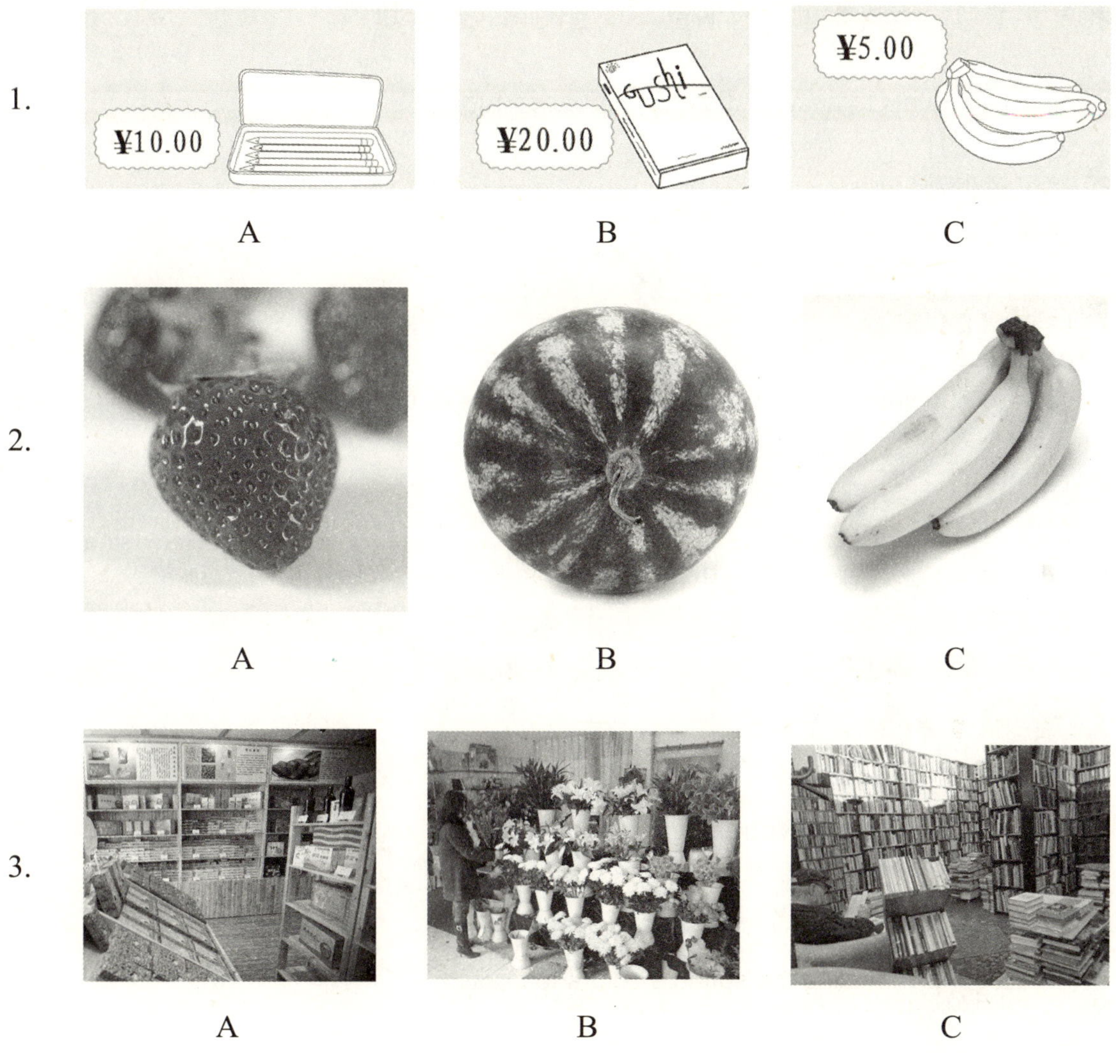

选择答案

Choose the correct responses to the sentences you have heard twice.

4. (　　) A 是的。B 是黄色的。C 我喜欢红色。
5. (　　) A 很好。B 是黄色的。C 有。
6. (　　) A 一个。B 两个。　C 两块。

Speaking

听后回答

Listen to your teacher carefully, then answer the questions.

Read a shopping plan twice. These things should be included in the shopping plan followed by their prices:

苹果　香蕉　牛奶　包子　书　书包　铅笔

For example：

我要买书包。我喜欢黄色的书包。黄色的书包五十块钱。

Then ask students to answer these questions in turn.

1. 老师要买什么？
2. 书包多少钱？
3. 老师喜欢什么颜色的书包？

购物 Shopping

The teacher takes the role of a seller. Each student should come to the teacher and pretend to buy something. The teacher encourages students to speak in Chinese more.

Reading

选择答案

Choose the correct answers to the questions in the left column.

1. 你要买什么？	☐	A 红色。
2. 你喜欢什么颜色？	☐	B 买书包。
3. 多少钱？	☐	C 五十块。

选词填空

Complete the dialogues with the given words.

A 觉得　B 的　C 要

4. A：你（　　）买书吗？　B：不。
5. A：你（　　）这个书包怎么样？　B：很好。
6. A：我的新书包是绿色（　　）。　B：很漂亮。

Free Reading

Read the shopping plan, then answer the questions below.

乐乐要买小鱼。小鱼：5块钱。

妈妈要买面条。面条：8块钱。

爸爸要买书包。书包：90块钱。

Questions：

1. 乐乐要买什么？
2. 谁要买面条？
3. 爸爸买的书包多少钱？

UNIT 10

今天比昨天冷

LESSON OBJECTIVES

Language

Students will be able to

- Understand and use 比 to express comparison.
- Talk about weather briefly.

Culture

Students will be able to know about

- Talking about weather.

  Talking about weather is a common way to start a conversation in China, for both old friends and strangers. Here are some useful Chinese sentences:

  今天天气真好！It's a lovely day!

  要下雨了。It's going to rain.

  今天真冷啊！It's so cold!

  今天真热啊！It's so hot!

  天气真好！不冷不热。It is not very cold and not very hot. It's perfect.

- The climates of China.

  The climates of different cities in China vary widely. Here are some typical examples of the differences.

  12月9日

  哈尔滨　–15℃ — – 12℃

  北京　– 5℃ — 5℃

  上海　12℃ — 17℃

  海口　20℃ — 27℃

TEACHING TIP

It would be best if the teacher provides a map of China to show where these cities are located.

TARGET VOCABULARY AND SENTENCE STRUCTURE

Vocabulary

天气　　热　　冷　　比　　昨天

Sentence Structure

A比B(Adjective)。
A比B(Adjective)(quantity phrase)。

SUGGESTED ACTIVITIES

Guided Practice

- 比一比 Let's Compare

  Show some pictures of different Chinese cities and have students compare the weather with sentences using 比.

  For example: A比B热。
  B比A冷。

  TEACHING TIP
  Give some pictures of different cities to the students in groups, asking them to compare the weather.

- 今天、昨天和明天 Today, Yesterday and Tomorrow

  Give the calendar to students and help them find the dates of today, yesterday and tomorrow. For example:

  今天是12月24日，星期四。
  昨天是12月23日，星期三。
  明天是12月25日，星期五。

  Then find three volunteers. Have one choose a date randomly and define it as 今天, the others should say 昨天 and 明天 according to the definition.

• 好朋友 Good Friends
Begin this game first with this sentence:
老师：我有三个好朋友。（学生1的名字），你呢？
学生1：我有四个好朋友。
老师：你的好朋友比我多一个。

Then lead students in continuing this dialogue.
学生1：我有四个好朋友。（学生2的名字），你呢？
学生2：我有两个好朋友。
学生1：你的好朋友比我少两个。

• 听一听 Listening Workbook
Listen to your teacher and decide if the descriptions are true or false.
Read the Chinese sentences twice.
1. 昨天天气比今天冷。
2. Tom的手比贝贝的手小。
3. 贝贝起床比Tom早二十分钟。
4. 中国大，日本小。
5. 我觉得，你的汉语比我好。

TEACHING TIP
The teacher leads students to compare their hands in pairs first. Then ask them to draw their hands on the page and form a sentence using 比 in Chinese.

• 写写说说 Let's Trace and Say Workbook
Prepare some flashcard to present the right stroke order of 比. Then ask students to trade and read this character.
比 - ⺊ ⺊ 比（横、竖提、撇、竖弯钩）

• 画一画 Let's Draw Workbook
Put your hands on the left page and draw it. Then ask your partner to put out his/her hands on the right page and draw it, too. Then compare them.

• 观察与判断 Observe and Judge Workbook
Observe the information in the picture. Then compare the persons on their ages.

TEACHING TIP
The teacher divides the class in several groups, asking students to talk about the questions in groups then declare the conclusion of each group before the class.

Independent Practice

- 讨论 Free Talking
  Divide the class into groups (5-6 students in each group), asking them to talk about the weather of their hometown in this season and get a conclusion, finding which places are colder and which places are hotter .

- 接球问答 Get the Ball and Answer My Question
  The teacher asks a question with比. For example:
  （学生1的名字），哥哥比你大几岁？
  The student who gets the ball should say:
  哥哥比我大一岁。/我没有哥哥。

  If he/she answers the questions in Chinese correctly and quickly, he/she will earn the chance to throw the ball and ask others a question with 比.

- 耳语 Whispers
  Whisper to the first student in each line:
  我的朋友比你多。
  今天的天气比昨天热。
  我的手比你的手大。
  我觉得红色比黄色漂亮。

- 数一数 Let's Count Workbook
  Count the numbers of the pencils. Fill in the blanks with the numbers. Then get a conclusion.
  Ask some students to read their conclusions.

- 回答问题 Answer the Questions Workbook
  Answer the questions according to the text, then give a correct order of their ages.

TEACHING TIP
Ask students to bring their reports to the class and give a presentation.

- 天气调查 A Survey of Weather Workbook

Find out temperature information in three cities. Then compare them to reach a conclusion.

- 我的故事书 My Story Book
  Ask students to make a story book which concerns some interesting experiences in cold or hot weather.

- 讲故事 Story Telling
  Ask students to recount some sentences based on the pictures.

- 唱一唱 Let's Sing **Workbook**
  Have students practice this song in pairs. Then perform before the whole class and elect the best partners.

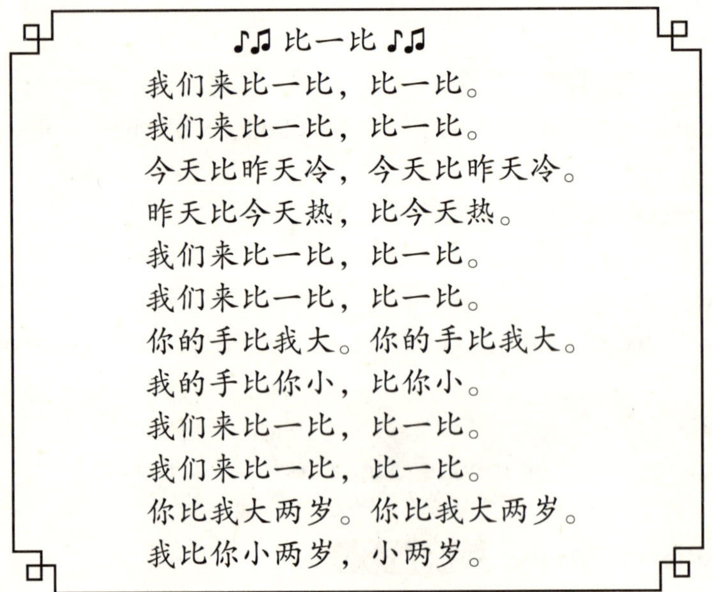

♪♫ 比一比 ♪♫

我们来比一比，比一比。
我们来比一比，比一比。
今天比昨天冷，今天比昨天冷。
昨天比今天热，比今天热。
我们来比一比，比一比。
我们来比一比，比一比。
你的手比我大。你的手比我大。
我的手比你小，比你小。
我们来比一比，比一比。
我们来比一比，比一比。
你比我大两岁。你比我大两岁。
我比你小两岁，小两岁。

Question for Reflection

What kind of clothes would you take if you planned to visit Beijing in December?

TEACHING TIP

Show some pictures of the winter in Beijing before students answer this question.

ASSESSMENT

Listening

选择图片

Choose the pictures corresponding to the sentences you have heard twice.

A

B

C

1. □
2. □
3. □

选择答案

Choose the correct answers to the questions you have heard twice.

4.	(　　) A 今天我去学校。	B 今天星期一。	C 今天很热。
5.	(　　) A 是。	B 好。	C 有。
6.	(　　) A 姐姐叫 Susan。	B 姐姐比我大五岁。	C 姐姐今年十六岁。

Speaking

听后回答

Listen to the recording carefully then answer the questions.

Prepare a recent weather forecast in Chinese. Ask students to listen and answer these questions in turn.

1. 北京的天气怎么样?
2. 北京比我们这儿冷吗?
3. 我们这儿比北京热吗?

看图说话

Describe the picture in Chinese.

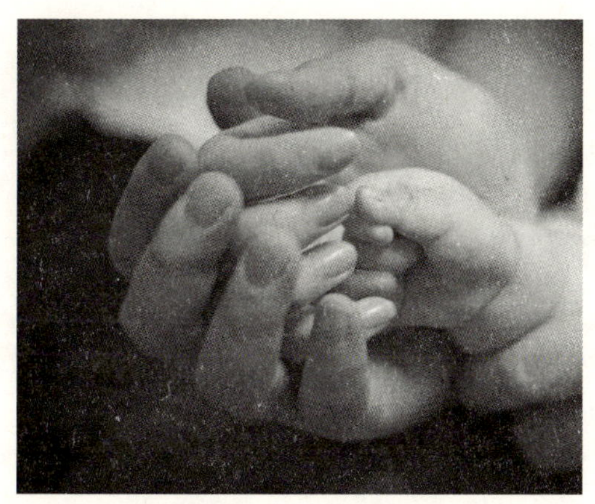

Reading

选择答案

Choose the correct response according to the sentences in the left column.

1. 这是谁的书？ ☐ A 大两岁。
2. 李心爱比Tom大几岁？ ☐ B 王贝贝的。
3. 明天的天气怎么样？ ☐ C 比今天冷。

选词填空

Complete the dialogues with the given words.

A不　　B 比　　C 的

4. A：我觉得红色（　　）黄色好看。B：是吗？
5. A：你比他大吗？ B：（　　），他比我大。
6. A：这是你的书包吗？ B：这是姐姐的书包，我（　　）是绿色的。

Free Reading

Read the weather forecast below then answer the questions.

昨天的天气很冷。今天的天气比昨天好。

明天的天气怎么样呢？

明天的天气不冷也不热。

Questions：

1. 昨天的天气冷吗？
2. 今天的天气怎么样？
3. 明天的天气好吗？

UNIT 11

你怎么了

LESSON OBJECTIVES

Language

Students will be able to

- Express concern with 你怎么了.
- Describe symptoms simply.
- Understand and use the modal verb 可以.

Culture

Students will be able to understand

- TCM

  TCM is Traditional Chinese Medicine which has thousands years of history. It involves an understanding of the human body and diseases that is different from western medicine by emphasizing integral treatment, considering the body a meridian system that could be adjusted.

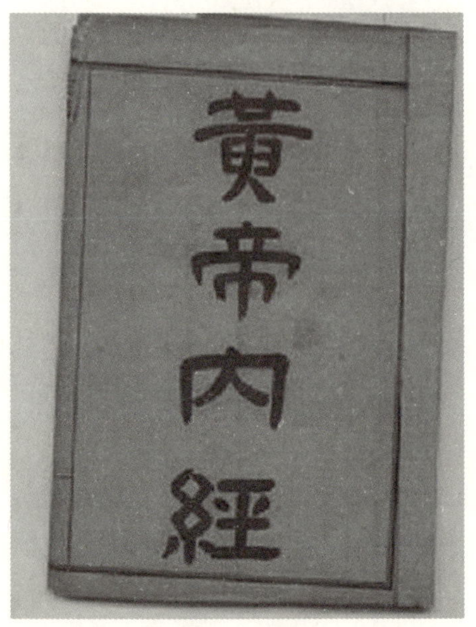

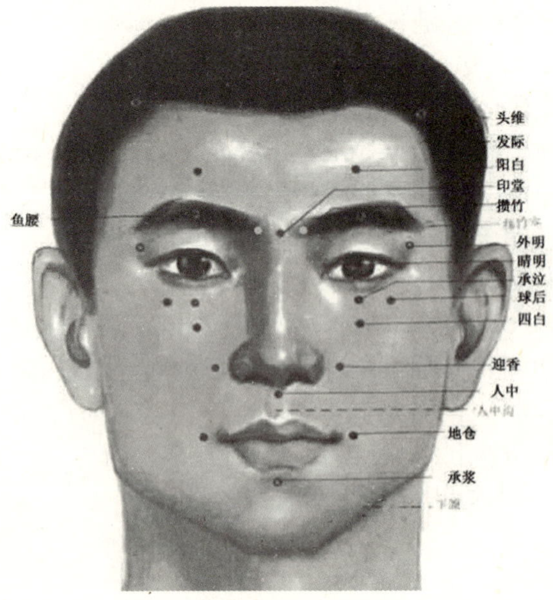

- Natural medicine of TCM.
  Traditional Chinese Medicine is mainly from plants, a few coming from animals. These materials are natural without artificial additives. The art of the medicine lies in matching them in well-formed combinations.

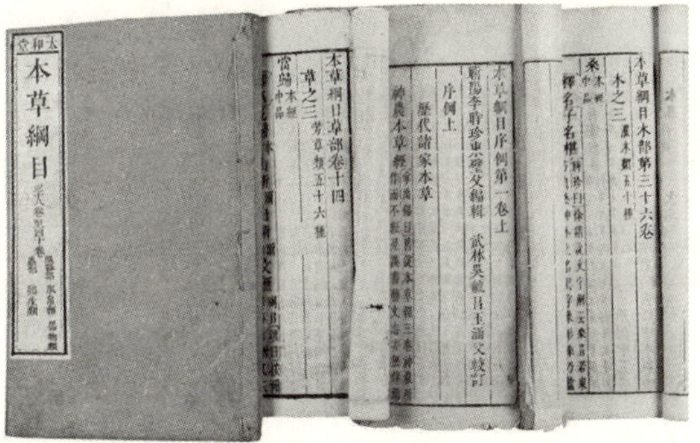

TARGET VOCABULARY AND SENTENCE STRUCTURE

Vocabulary

可以	怎么	医院	说话
张口	电视	脚	

Sentence Structure

你怎么了？
我的头很热。
我可以(action)吗？

SUGGESTED ACTIVITIES

Guided Practice

- 字卡游戏 Character Cards Game

- 快速反应 Respond Quickly

  Ask some volunteers to show this game. They should point to a body part when the teacher says the name of the part in Chinese. The teacher should say the body parts quickly — it will amuse students if someone points to the wrong part or can't keep up.

  Ask the whole class to play this game together. At last find some volunteers to say the words and the teacher will follow up their orders with the other students together.

- 你怎么了 What's Wrong with You

  Ask a volunteer to act out some uncomfortable situations. Have the other students to guess what's wrong with him/her, saying these sentences:

  （名字），你怎么了？
  你的头很热？
  你的脚很疼？

  The volunteer can't tell other students his/her symptoms directly. He/she should continue performing if the others don't understand.

TEACHING TIP

The teacher can provide some new words helping students to express symptoms，such as 肚子(belly)，疼(painful).

- 选一选 Let's Choose **Workbook**

  Choose the pictures that match to the dialogues.

TEACHING TIP

Have students observe the pictures carefully, and understand when Chinese people would use the sentence 你怎么了. For example, this sentence appears when somebody looks very uncomfortable, sad or angry.

- 观察与连线 Observe and Match **Workbook**

  Observe the pictures then match them to the proper sentences.

- 听听连连 Listen and Match **Workbook**

  Match the responses to the situations corresponding to what you have heard. Read these sentences twice.

  ｛你怎么了？
  ｛我头疼。

{不要说话，张口！
啊……

{多喝点水？
好的。

{我可以看电视吗？
可以，要少看！

{谢谢您，医生！
不客气！

- 观察与判断 Observe and Judge **Workbook**
  There are five mistakes hiding in this picture. Try to find them and circle them, then explain why they are wrong in Chinese.

> **TEACHING TIP**
> Ask students to observe the pictures in groups and organize a composition for checking mistakes. Then lead each group to explain the reasons in Chinese and say the right answers.

Independent Practice

- 西蒙说 Simon Says
  Ask students to stand in a big circle and play this game. The one whose role is Simon should use these words for body parts when he/she gives order to others. For example:
  Simon 说：鼻子/手/脚/胳膊/眼睛/耳朵
  Simon 说：张口！/看电视！/多喝水！/多睡觉！

- 说一说 Let's Talk **Workbook**
  Say something about this picture in Chinese with your partner.
  Students will have a free conversation on the following topics:
  她是谁？
  他是谁？
  她在哪儿？
  她怎么了？
  他说什么？

- 写写说说 Let's Trace and Speak **Workbook**
  Prepare some flashcards to present the structure and the stroke order of 口, then encourage students to write and read it.

- 耳语 Whispers
  Whisper to the first student in each line:
  我的头很热。
  我觉得很冷。
  妈妈的脚很疼。
  不要说话！
  多喝水！

- 医生和病人 Doctors and Patients
  Ask students to decorate their classroom. Students are divided to three groups freely, one group takes the roles of doctors, one acts as patients and the third group provides consulting services.

- 可以不可以 Can or Can Not
  Students practice the dialogue with 可以 in pairs. For example:
  我可以看电视吗？
  可以。/不可以。

  我可以看你的书吗？
  可以。/不可以。

- 课本剧表演 Perform A Script
  Put four students in each group. Act out the script. After practicing, act in turn and choose the best team.

- 唱一唱 Let's Sing **Workbook**
  Have students practice this song in groups, and then select the best team.

♪♫ 你怎么了 ♪♫

你怎么了？我的朋友。
你不快乐吗？不快乐吗？
你的头很热，头很热。
我们去医院吧，去医院吧。
你怎么了？我的朋友。
你这是怎么了？怎么了？
你的头很热，头很热。
我们去医院吧，去医院吧。
你怎么了？我的朋友。
我们去医院，去医院吧。

Question for Reflection

What would you say if you are asked to introduce the TCM?

TEACHING TIP

Show some pictures of TCM to students and ask them to design a brief introduction of TCM in groups. Then present their reports in class.

ASSESSMENT

Listening

选择图片

Choose the pictures corresponding to the sentences you have heard twice.

A

B

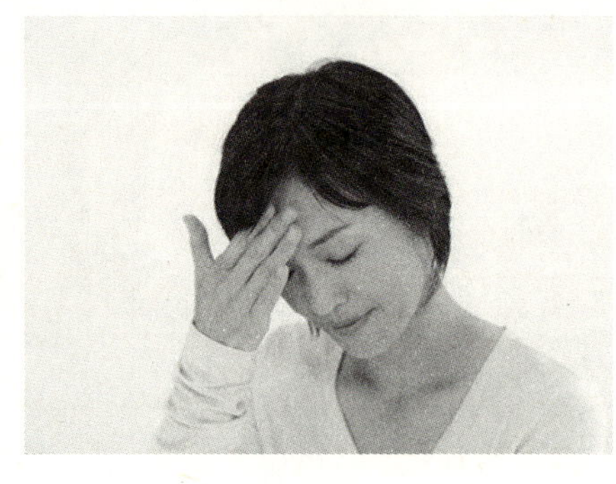

C

1. ☐
2. ☐
3. ☐

选择答案

Choose the correct answers according to the questions you have heard twice.

4. (　　) A Tom是美国人。B Tom九岁了。 C Tom的头很热。
5. (　　) A 多看电视。　B 少看电视。　C 少喝水。
6. (　　) A 妈妈在家。　B 妈妈去医院。C 好多了。

Speaking

听后回答

Listen to your teacher carefully then answer the questions.

Read the sentences twice. Ask students to listen and answer these questions in turn.

Suggested sentences:

Tom今天没有去学校，他和妈妈去医院了。

Tom的头很热。

医生说：多喝水，多睡觉！少看电视！

Questions:

1. Tom怎么了？
2. Tom去哪儿了？
3. 医生说什么？

讲故事

Tell a story according to the pictures.

A

B

C

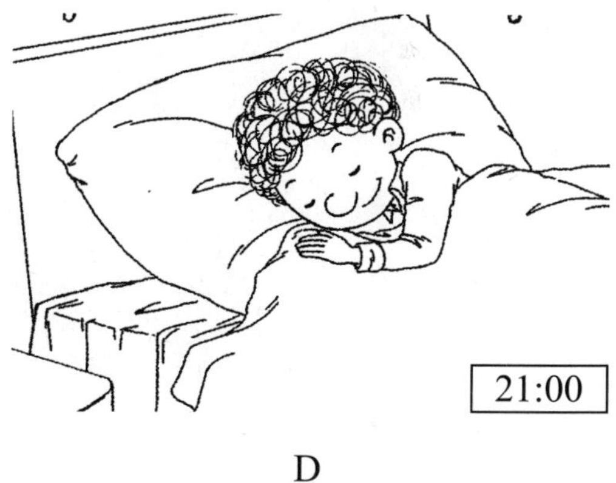

D

Reading

选择答案

Choose the correct response to the sentences in the left column.

1. 我可以喝茶吗？	□	A 不客气！
2. 你怎么了？	□	B 可以。
3. 我好多了，谢谢您！	□	C 我觉得很冷。

选词填空

Complete the dialogues with the given words.

A怎么　　B 吧　　C 可以

1. A：你（　　）了？　　B：我的小猫不见了！

2. A：医生，我（　　）看书吗？B：要少看！

3. A：我的脚……　　B：我们去医院（　　）！

Free Reading

Read Tom's diary carefully then answer the questions.

今天星期二，我没有去学校。早上，我觉得头很热，脚很冷。妈妈和我去医院了。医生说："多睡觉！少看电视！"我很喜欢看电视。今天晚上我不看电视，我要多睡觉。

Questions：

1. 今天星期几？
2. Tom怎么了？
3. Tom今天晚上看电视吗？

UNIT 12

你做什么呢

LESSON OBJECTIVES

Language

Students will be able to

- Understand the usage of the modal particle 呢：to express an action is going on and convey a close feeling.
- Notice this usage of 呢 after the verb phrases.
- Review some words and structures that students have learned before.

Culture

Students will be able to know about

- Internet language in China.

  Chinese young people love to keep in touch with each other on the Internet as the ones in other countries nowadays. They even created some special signals which can be used just on the internet. For example, some difficult Chinese characters like 囧, expressing embarrassment; some numbers like 88, expressing goodbye; some sentences like "jiàngzǐ 酱紫（no real meaning）" which represents "zhèyàngzi 这样子（in this way）". They feel it's funny when they use these special words or sentences on the internet as they don't use them in formal essays or exams. However, the influences of internet language are increasing gradually.

小月 9:31:47
亲爱的，好久不见。明天一起吃饭吧。
Sandy 9:32:58
嗯……吃饭啊？
我正减肥呢，最近又长胖了……囧
小月 9:33:27
酱紫啊！那明天一起游泳，好不好？
Sandy 9:33:45
那好啊！明天见。88
小月 9:33:50
88

- Recommended places for travel.
  There are many good places worthy of visiting when you travel in China. Here are some recommended cities.

Beijing北京

Sanya 三亚

Shanghai 上海

Xi'an 西安

Lijiang 丽江

TEACHING TIP

The teacher can provide more pictures or videos of these beautiful places if students want to know more. The teacher can also provide some useful words for famous cities in China, such as 上海, 西安 and 丽江.

TARGET VOCABULARY AND SENTENCE STRUCTURE

Vocabulary

做　　　　海南

Notice：海南 is an additional word here.

Sentence Structure

(pepole)在(place)(action)呢。

SUGGESTED ACTIVITIES

Guided Practice

- 北京在哪儿 Where's Beijing

  Provide a map of China, asking students to find places which are mentioned. Students who know the position of a given city should stand before the map and point at the place with saying 在这儿.

  老师：北京在哪儿？
  学生1：老师，北京在这儿！

  老师：海南在哪儿？
  学生2：老师，海南在这儿！

TEACHING TIP

Provide other famous cities in China and practice more.

- 天气怎么样 How Is the Weather

  Divide the class into several groups. Provide the pictures of different cities with the information about weather, asking students to observe the weather information then arrive conclusions in groups, then organize a competition.

  老师：海南的天气怎么样?
  学生：海南的天气很热。
  老师：海南比（other city in China or the local city in U.S.A.）热吗?
  学生：海南比（the city that the teacher mentioned）热。

- 有趣的句子 Interesting Sentences

  Provide different components of a sentence then combine them randomly to get some reasonable or unreasonable sentences.

  Step1: Divide students into four groups, giving the first group some cards with time words, the second some cards of places, the third some cards of people and the last group some cards of actions.
  Step2: Four students, each from one group will reach their goal by putting the words together in correct order. They should stand before the class, holding their word cards and trying to find the exact words' order, then read the sentence aloud.
  Step 3: Have the whole class read the sentence again — some interesting sentences will be funny. For example: Tom在商店睡觉。

- 连一连 Match Workbook

  Match the phrases to the corresponding pictures.
  Have students match them and read the phrases.

- 写写说说 Let's Trace and Say

  Prepare some flashcards to present the stroke order of 冷, then ask students to trade and read this character.

- 听听做做 Listen and Act

  Listen to your teacher carefully then perform the actions which the teacher said.

  The teacher says the sentences twice, asking the whole class to stand up and perform the actions.

  做饭呢　　吃包子呢　　看书呢　　说话呢
  看电视呢　　睡觉呢　　喝水呢　　玩儿呢

- 去中国旅行 Travel in China

  Provide some brief introductions about famous places in China. Then ask students to choose a place as their destination in groups. Each group should provide a travel plan including the weather information, personal luggage, the persons they prefer to go with and so on.

> **TEACHING TIP**
> Show some videos or pictures of travelling in China before students do this activity.

Independent Practice

- 说一说 Let's Talk Workbook

  Say something about the weather of these two cities.

  The following sentences are recommended:

  北京的天气怎么样？
  北京很冷。

  北京比海南冷？
  海南比北京热。

- 调查与讨论 Survey and Talk Workbook

  Look for information on tomorrow's weather in Beijing, Haikou (the capital city of Hainan) and the city in which you are.

  The teacher asks students to bring their reports to the class and discuss the suggested topics in pairs.

  Suggested topics：

  明天北京的天气怎么样？

  那儿冷吗？

- 接球问答 Get the Ball and Answer My Question

  The teacher begins this game and asks a question with呢. For example:

  老师：你看，（学生名字1）做什么呢？

  The student who gets the ball should say: （学生名字1）在……呢。

  Other students can pretend to do something when their names are mentioned.

  If the student answers the questions in Chinese correctly and quickly, he/she will earn the chance to throw the ball and ask others a question with the same pattern.

- 耳语 Whispers

  Whisper to the first student in each line:

  （学生名字1）在说话呢。

（学生名字2）在家做饭呢。
（学生名字3）在看电视呢。
（学生名字4）在睡觉呢。
When the last student in each line speaks the sentence aloud, the ones whose names are mentioned should mime the actions. The students responding correctly and quickly will receive a small gift from the teacher.

TEACHING TIP
Use the real names of students and speak the names clearly enough to the first student in each line.

- 讲故事 Story Telling Workbook
  Recount the story presented in the picture.

  Divide the class into groups to practice and have each group elect one person to tell the story before the class.

TEACHING TIP
Provide some useful words：画(to draw), 喝(to drink), 玩(to play), 学习(to study), 说话(to say).

- 我的旅行纪念册 My Travel Book
  Ask students to make a book of their travelling experiences, then bring it to the class and talk about it with their team members. The weather, the food, the date they travelled and the persons they went with would be suitable topics.

- 上网聊天儿 Chatting on the Internet Workbook
  Ask students to chat with 3 classmates after class, asking them the same question 你做什么呢. Then finish this interview form.

- 唱一唱 Let's Sing Workbook
  Students practice the song in pairs and in two groups. Then select the best team.

♪♫ 你做什么呢 ♪♫

你做什么呢，Tom?
我吃饭呢，我吃饭呢！
你做什么呢，Linda?
我玩儿呢，我玩儿呢！
你做什么呢，贝贝？
我画画呢，我画画呢！
你做什么呢，心爱？
我做饭呢，我做饭呢！
你做什么呢，和子？
我学习呢，我学习呢！
你做什么呢？你做什么呢？
我唱歌呢，我唱歌呢！
啦啦啦啦，啦啦啦啦啦啦啦，
啦啦啦啦，啦啦啦啦啦啦啦。

TEACHING TIP

Ask students to perform this song by taking different roles and replace the names with their real name.

Question for Reflection

Which place in China would you want to visit? Why? What is it like there?

TEACHING TIP

Introduce some famous cities or places in China with videos or pictures before students answer this question.

ASSESSMENT

Listening

选择图片

Choose the pictures corresponding to the sentences you have heard twice.

A

B

C

1. □
2. □
3. □

选择答案

Choose the correct answers to the questions you have heard twice.

4. (　　) A 很热。　B 很好。　C 在这儿。
5. (　　) A 北京比海南冷。B 北京很热。　C 北京很大。
6. (　　) A 我很高兴。　B 我有一个好朋友。C 我和朋友说话呢。

Speaking

观察并回答

Provide some pictures or videos that depict somebody doing something. Ask students to observe carefully, and then answer these questions in turn.

Questions:

他/她做什么呢?

他们做什么呢?

讲故事

Tell a story based on the pictures.

北京，Tom家。窗外有雪。

海南，海滩上。

Reading

选词填空

Complete the dialogues with the given words.

A 在　　　B 呢　　　C 比

1. A：你做什么（　　）？B：我学习汉语。
2. A：贝贝呢？　　　　　B：他（　　）海南玩儿呢！
3. A：海南的天气怎么样？B：海南（　　）北京热多了！

Free Reading

A Instructions：Independent Practice "My Travel Book" can be used as a rubric for assessment here. Ask students to exchange the interesting things in the books.

B Instructions：Read Beibei's diary carefully then answer the questions.

现在我在海南。海南的天气比北京热多了！这儿有很多人。我和爸爸妈妈来海南玩儿。我的好朋友没有来。我喜欢大海，也喜欢海南。我很快乐！

Questions：

1. 贝贝在哪儿？__________。
2. 海南怎么样？____________。
3. 贝贝喜欢海南吗？____________。

Appendix Games

字卡游戏 CHARACTER CARDS GAME

This is a good way to emphasize the impression of Chinese characters. And students will get to know how to combine words with different characters.

Preparation

Prepare the character cards for this lesson.

Game play

The teacher demonstrates the correct words with these cards while reading the words.

The teacher gives students 5-8 minutes to remember the words.

The words are presented in two columns, one is a monosyllabic word and the other is a two-syllable word.

Then shuffle the cards. Students should try to get all of the words with the character cards while reading the words aloud. The group who can get more right words will be the winner.

拍词游戏 FLY SWATTERS

This is a fun game to review new vocabulary.

Preparation

Prepare a visual of the vocabulary pictures.

Game play

Students are divided into two teams and line up in two lines. The first person in each line has a fly swatter.

The teacher says one vocabulary item, the person who hits the visual first wins one point for the team.

师生竞赛 TEACHER VERSUS STUDENTS

This is a quick and fun way to review vocabulary when students are just beginning to learn them. Students become familiar with pronunciation and master the vocabulary while teacher says the word over and over again.

Preparation

Prepare a visual of the vocabulary pictures.

Game play

When the teacher points to a picture and says the correct word in Chinese, all the students should "chorally" repeat the word.

If the teacher says the wrong word in Chinese, all the students should remain silent.

If all the students remain silent when the teacher is "wrong", they receive a point. If any student starts to repeat the wrong word, the teacher receives the point.

猜一猜 GUESS THE WORDS

This is a fun game to recognize the meanings of the vocabulary, especially for the verbs of verb phrases.

Preparation

The teacher provides the volunteers some target vocabulary.

Game play

Ask a volunteer to choose a word and act out the meaning of it.

Other students try to guess the Chinese word and say the words aloud.

One should keep performing if others don't understand.

西蒙说 SIMON SAYS

This is a fun way to review vocabulary. It's a game for at least three persons. One of the players is chosen as Simon. The others must do what Simon tells them to do when asked with a phrase beginning with "Simon says".

If Simon says "Simon says 请坐", the players must sit down. However, if Simon says simply "请坐", without saying "Simon says", players do not sit down.

The last of Simon's followers to stay in wins.

TEACHING TIP

Add the real names of students into Simon's orders to make this game more challenging and fun. For example:

Tom，请坐！/ Simon says, Tom, 请坐！

字—词—句 CHARACTERS—WORDS—SENTENCES

This is designed for paying attention to the word order of Chinese and practicing how to get a sentence structure as well.

Preparation

Prepare enough character cards.

Game play

Divide the class in groups, each group including 5 at least.

Everyone gets a character card and should find the others to assemble words and sentences quickly.

The group which forms most words and sentences will be the winner.

The winner should present the words and sentences by standing in a row while holding the cards in the correct order.

Other students read the sentences aloud and check if they are correct or not.

耳语 WHISPERS

This is a good and fun way to repeat the target sentence structures. Students are required to convey a whispered message one by one in order to convey a sentence which the teacher says to the first person in each line.

Preparation

The teacher chooses some target sentence structures.

Game play

Group the students into teams and ask them stand in lines.

The teacher whispers to the first student in each line with different sentences.

Students whisper the sentence to the student behind them. The last student in each line speaks the sentence aloud.

The team that ends up with the exact sentence wins this game.

接球问答 GET THE BALL AND ANSWER MY QUESTION

This is a fun game to review the dialogues and practice them in real situation.

Preparation

Prepare a colorful ball or balloon.

Game play

The teacher throws a soft ball to some student. After the student catches the ball, ask some questions.

Students who can answer the questions in Chinese correctly and quickly will earn the chance to throw the ball and ask others.

有趣的句子 INTERESTING SENTENCES

This is a fun way to review the target sentence structures. Students provide different components of a sentence then combine them randomly to get some reasonable or unreasonable sentences.

Game play

Divide students into four groups, giving the first group some cards with time words, the second some cards of places, the third some cards of people and the last group some cards of actions.

Four students from each the four groups will reach their goal by putting the words together in correct order. They should stand before the class, holding their word cards and trying to find the exact words order then read the sentence aloud.

Have the whole class read the sentence again. Some interesting sentences will be funny. For example: Tom 在商店睡觉。

课本剧表演 PERFORM A SCRIPT

This is a good and fun activity to review the contents of texts. Students will be asked to speak the sentences by themselves and act the script out creatively.

Put three to five students in one group (according to the storyline). Act out the script. After practicing, perform in turns and choose the best team.

讨论 FREE TALKING

This is a good way to encourage students to speak Chinese without too much stress. Students can use their native language or ask for the teacher's help when they don't know how to express some ideas in Chinese.

Divide the class into groups (5-6 students in each group). Give them the main topic in Chinese. Let them talk about it freely. Then have each group sum up and present their own opinion with Chinese as more as possible.

思考 QUESTION FOR REFLECTION

This is a good chance to remind students the main cultural factors that they have learned. Or let students get their opinions through positive reflection.

TEACHING TIP

The teacher provides some videos or pictures to present the cultural themes more vividly.

YCT-Friendly Tests

Units 1–6

一、听力

第一部分

第1-5题

例如：

✓

×

1.

2.

3.

4.

5.

第二部分

第6-10题

A

B

C

D

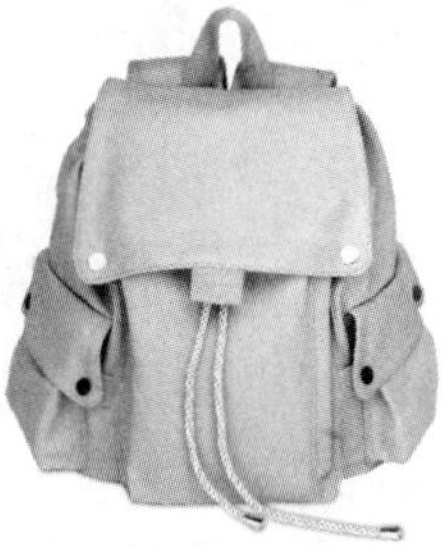

E

F

Wǒ de māma shì yīshēng.
例如：我 的 妈妈 是 医生。 [C]

6. ☐

7. ☐

8. ☐

9. ☐

10. ☐

第三部分

第11-15题

例如：			
	A	B ✓	C
11.			
	A	B	C
12.			
	A	B	C
13.			
	A	B	C

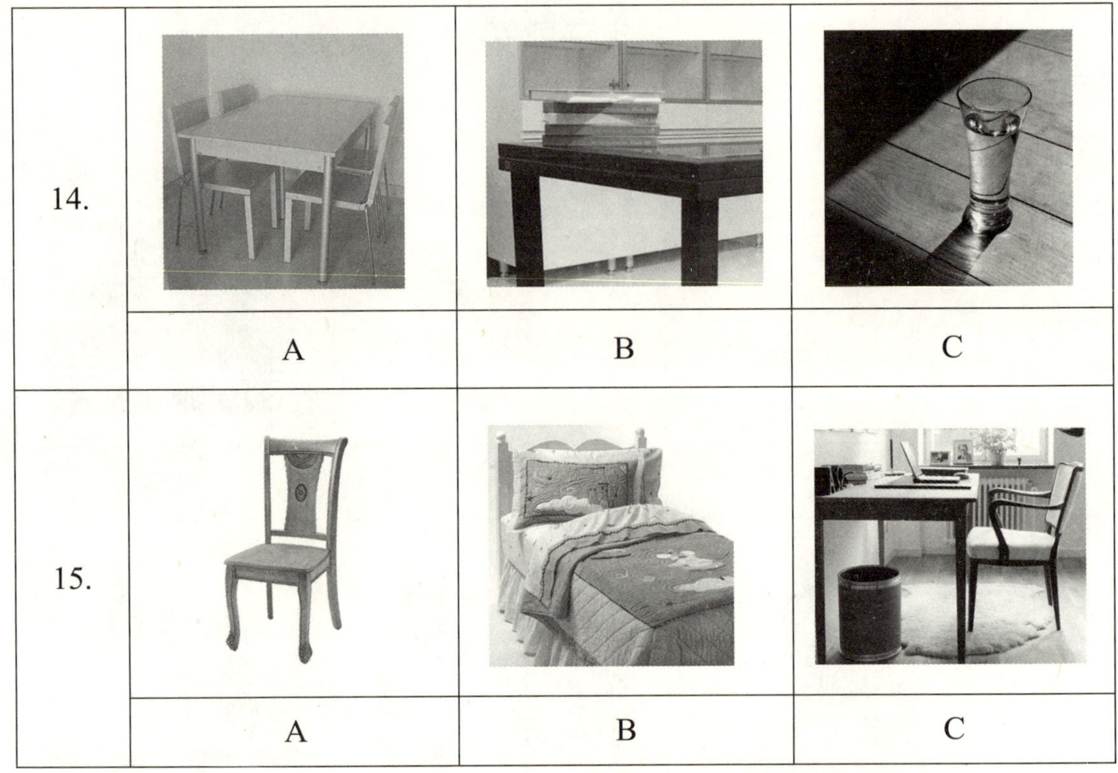

第四部分

第16-20题

例如：你的家在哪儿？(Nǐ de jiā zài nǎr?)

A 我叫王贝贝。(Wǒ jiào Wáng Bèi bei) B 在北京。(Zài Běijīng) ✓ C 九岁。(Jiǔ suì)

16. A 对不起。(Duìbuqǐ) B 没关系。(Méi guānxi) C 不客气。(Búkèqi)

17. A 她是美国人。(Tā shì Měiguórén) B 来了。(Lái le) C 请坐。(Qǐng zuò)

18. A 好。(Hǎo) B 谢谢。(Xièxie) C 会。(Huì)

19. A 真漂亮。(Zhēn piàoliang) B 我学习中国画三个月了。(Wǒ xuéxí Zhōngguóhuà sāngè yuè le) C 没关系。(Méi guānxi)

20. A 我来了。(Wǒ lái le) B 认识你很高兴。(Rènshi nǐ hěn gāoxìng) C 好的。(Hǎode)

二、阅读

第一部分

第21-25题

例如：	 huàhuàr 画画儿　×		 sì zhī qiānbǐ 四 只 铅笔　✓
21.	 Běijīng 北京	22.	 duìbuqǐ 对不起
23.	 wǒ huì huàhuàr 我 会 画画儿	24.	 dǎ diànhuà 打 电话
25.	 xióngmāo 熊猫		

第二部分

第26-30题

A 

B 

C 

D 

E 

F 

Huà shàng yǒu shénme? Huà shàng yǒu liǎng zhī xiǎogǒu.

例如：A：画上有什么？ B：画上有两只小狗。 [B]

Māma, lái! Nǐ de diànhuà!

26. A：妈妈，来！你的电话！ □

Wǒ lái le.

B：我来了。

Qǐng zuò!

27. A：请坐！ □

Xièxiè!
B：谢谢！

Zhuōzi shàngbian yǒu shénme?
28．A：桌子 上边 有 什么？ ☐

Zhuōzi shàngbian yǒu shū hé chá.
B：桌子 上边 有 书 和 茶。

Tā jǐ suì?
29．A：他几岁？ ☐

Tā wǔ suì.
B：他 五 岁。

Zhè shì wǒ huà de Zhōngguóhuà, zěnmeyàng?
30．A：这 是 我 画 的 中国画， 怎么样？ ☐

Zhēn piàoliang!
B：真 漂亮！

第三部分

第31-35题

例如：Fángjiān lǐ yǒu jǐ gè rén? 房间 里有 几个 人？	E	A	Wǒ huì. 我 会。
31. Wǒ jīnnián shíjiǔ suì, nǐ ne? 我 今年 十九 岁，你 呢？	☐	B	Rènshi nǐ hěn gāoxìng. 认识 你很 高兴。
32. Zhēn duìbuqǐ! 真 对不起！	☐	C	Hǎo de. 好 的。
33. Nǐ huìbuhuì shuō Hànyǔ? 你 会不会 说 汉语？	☐	D	Wǒ shí'èr suì. 我 十二 岁。
34. Xiǎogāo, zhè shì Měiměi. 小高， 这 是 美美。	☐	E	Liǎng gè rén. 两 个 人。
35. Wǒmen hēchá, hǎo ma? 我们 喝茶，好 吗？	☐	F	Méi guānxi. 没 关系。

第四部分

第36-40题

búkèqi qǐng zhēn yě lǐmiàn zhī
A 不客气　B 请　C 真　D 也　E 里面　F 只

Nǐ hǎo! zuò!
例如：A：你 好！（ B ）坐！

Xièxie nǐ!
B：谢谢 你！

Zhè gè fángjiān zěnmeyàng?
36. A：这 个 房间 怎么样？

piàoliang!
B：（　　）漂亮！

Wǒ xǐhuan Běijīng.
37. A：我 喜欢 北京。

Wǒ xǐhuan Běijīng.
B：我（　　）喜欢 北京。

Xièxie nǐ!
38. A：谢谢 你！

B：（　　）。

Kàn! Nàr yǒu xiǎoniǎo!
39. A：看！ 那儿 有 小鸟！

Nàr yǒu liǎng xiǎoniǎo.
B：那儿 有 两（　　）小鸟。

Nǐ de qiānbǐ ne?
40. A：你 的 铅笔 呢？

Zài shūbāo
B：在 书包（　　）。

Units 1−12

(Official Examination Paper of YCT Level 2)

一、听力

第一部分（第1-5题）

例如：

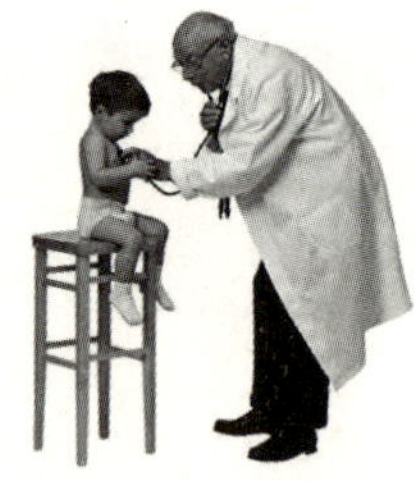

√ ×

1. 

2. 

3. 

4. 

5. 

第二部分（第6-10题）

A

B

C

D

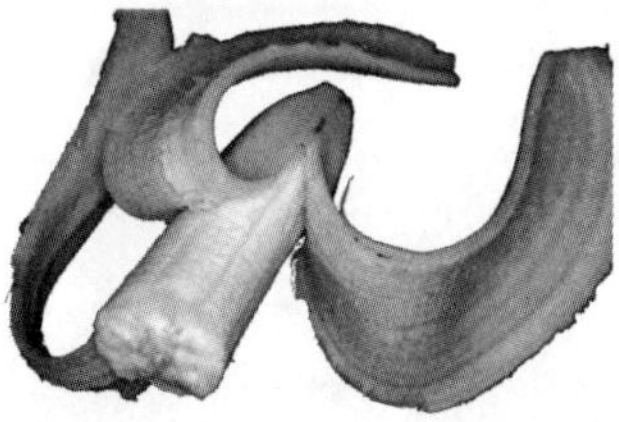

E

F

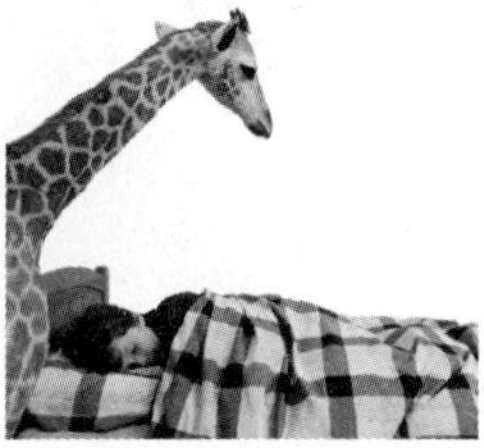

Nǐ shì hóngsè de, wǒ shì huángsè de.
例如：你是 红色 的，我 是 黄色 的。 C

6.

7.

8.

9.

10.

第三部分（第11-15题）

例如：			
	A	B	C ✓
11.			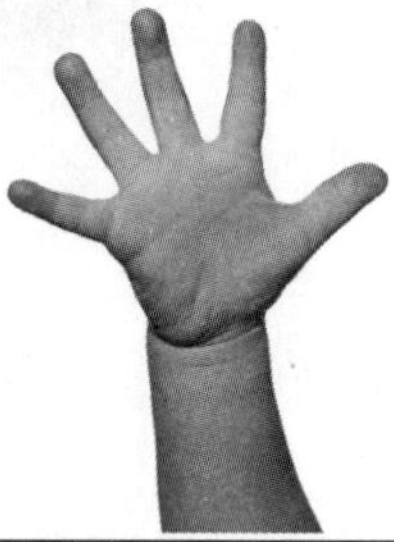
	A	B	C
12.			
	A	B	C
13.			
	A	B	C

14.	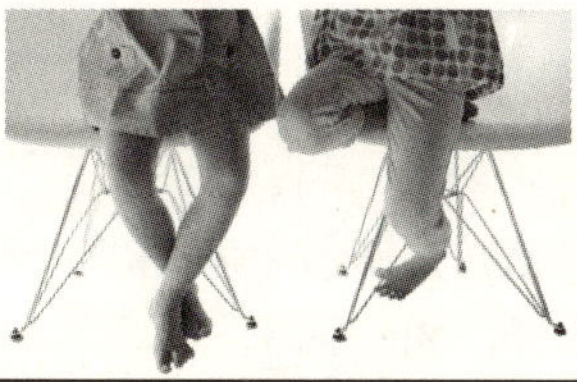		
	A	B	C
15.			
	A	B	C

第四部分（第16-20题）

Tā shì shéi?
例如：她是谁？

	A	B	C
	búkèqi A 不客气	qù yīyuàn B 去 医院	wǒ de xuésheng C 我 的 学生 ✓
16.	bú rè A 不 热	zhēn piàoliang B 真 漂亮	zài lǐmiàn C 在 里面
17.	wǒ rènshi A 我 认识	wǒ mèimei B 我 妹妹	qù xuéxiào le C 去 学校 了
18.	xièxie A 谢谢	jǐ gè yǐzi B 几 个 椅子	kěyǐ, qǐng zuò C 可以，请 坐
19.	Zhōngguórén A 中国人	duō gè B 50多 个	wǒmen de péngyou C 我们 的 朋友
20.	tā bú huì A 她 不 会	hěn hǎochī B 很 好吃	mǎile gè bāozi C 买了 4 个 包子

二、阅读

第一部分（第21-25题）

例如：	 kàn diànshì 看 电视 ×		 zhuōzi hé yǐzi 桌子 和 椅子✓
21.	 diǎn fēn 9点20分	22.	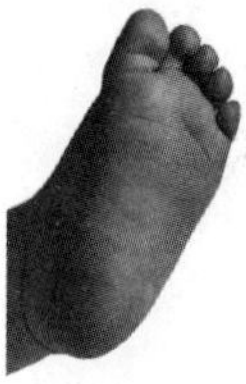 xiǎoniǎo de jiǎo 小鸟 的 脚
23.	 wǒ de yǎnjing 我 的 眼睛	24.	 dǎ diànhuà 打 电话
25.	 liǎng zhī yú 两 只 鱼		

第二部分（第26-30题）

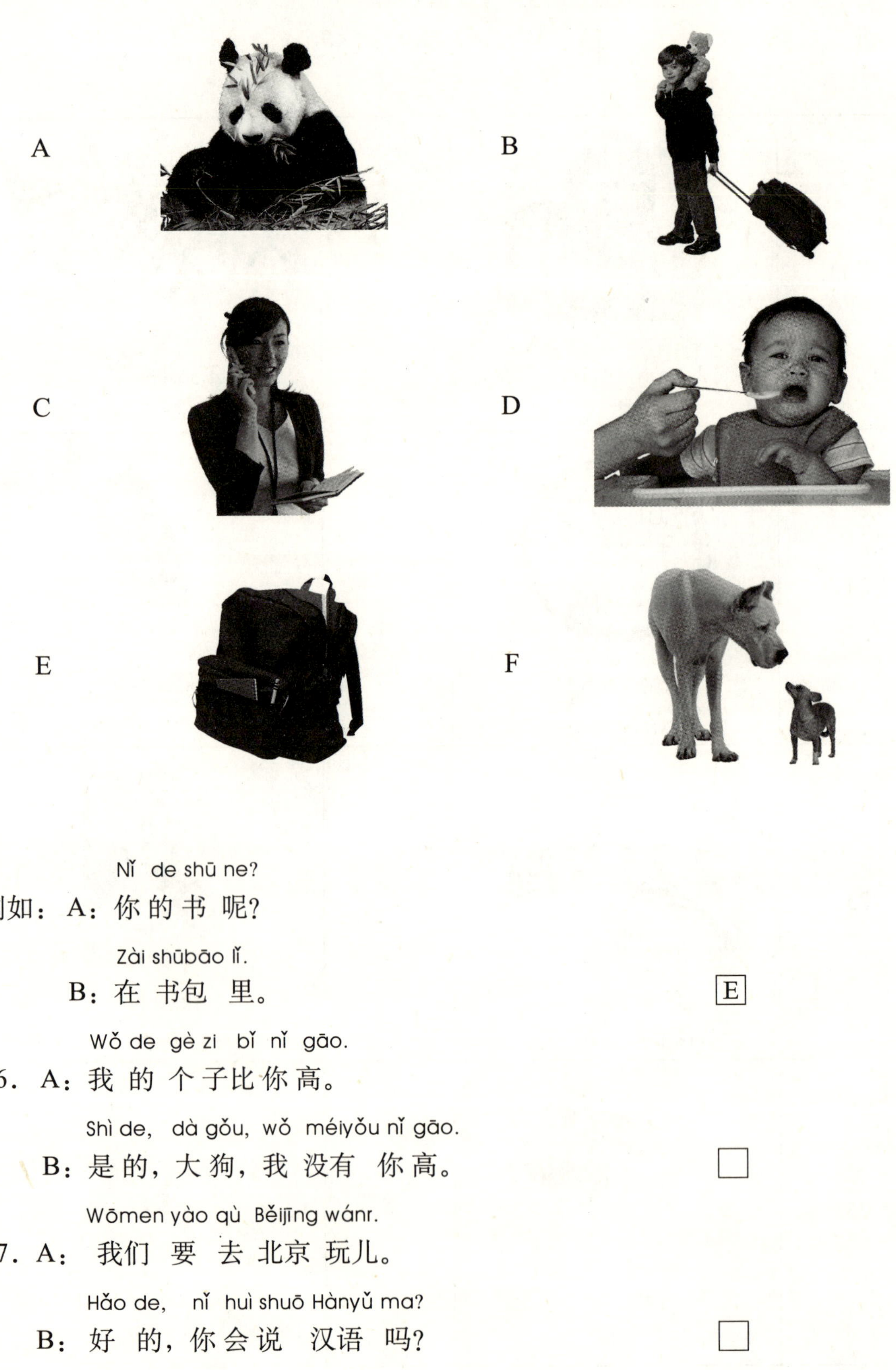

Nǐ de shū ne?
例如：A：你的书 呢？

Zài shūbāo lǐ.
B：在 书包 里。 E

Wǒ de gè zi bǐ nǐ gāo.
26．A：我 的 个 子比 你 高。

Shì de, dà gǒu, wǒ méiyǒu nǐ gāo.
B：是的，大 狗，我 没有 你 高。 ☐

Wǒmen yào qù Běijīng wánr.
27．A： 我们 要 去 北京 玩儿。

Hǎo de, nǐ huì shuō Hànyǔ ma?
B：好 的，你 会 说 汉语 吗？ ☐

Zhè zhī xióngmāo jīnnián jǐ suì le?

28. A：这 只 熊猫 今年 几 岁 了?

Yí suì líng liù gè yuè.

B：一岁 零 六 个 月。 □

Tā zěnme le?

29. A：他 怎么 了?

Méi guānxi, tā juéde zhège bù hǎochī.

B：没 关系，他 觉得 这个 不 好吃。 □

Lǐ lǎoshī shuō tā míngtiān diǎn lái.

30. A：李 老师 说 他 明天 8 点 来。

Hǎo, xièxie nǐ, zàijiàn.

B：好， 谢谢 你，再见。 □

第三部分（第31-35题）

例如：	Zhège qiānbǐ duōshao qián? 这个 铅笔 多少 钱？	D	A Tóngxué jiā. 同学 家。
31.	Zuótiān wǎnshang nǐ qù nǎr le? 昨天 晚上 你 去 哪儿 了？		B Bízi. 鼻子。
32.	Nǐ zài nǎge fángjiān ne? 你 在 哪个 房间 呢？		C Wǒ ài wánr. 我 爱 玩儿。
33.	Nǐ ài xuéxí ma? 你 爱 学习 吗？		D Sān kuài. 三 块。
34.	Nǐ xǐhuan shénme yánsè de shūbāo? 你 喜欢 什么 颜色 的 书包？		E Lǜ de. 绿 的。
35.	Kǒu de shàngbian shì shénme? 口 的 上边 是 什么？		F 207。

第四部分（第36-40题）

A	yīshēng 医生	B	zěnmeyàng 怎么样	C	míngzi 名字	D	huáng 黄	E	yě 也	F	rènshi 认识

Wǒ jiào Míngming, hěn gāoxìng nǐ。
例如：A：我 叫 明明， 很 高兴（ F ）你。

Míngming, nǐ hǎo! Wǒ jiào Fāngfang。
B：明明， 你 好！ 我 叫 芳芳。

Nǐ zài huà shénme?
36．A：你 在 画 什么？

Wǒ zài huà māo, zhè zhī māo shì sè de.
B：我 在 画 猫，这 只 猫 是（ ）色 的。

Wǒ dìdi bù xǐhuan hē niúnǎi.
37．A：我 弟弟 不 喜欢 喝 牛奶。

Wǒ shì.
B：我（ ）是。

Nǐ māma shì lǎoshī ma?
38．A：你 妈妈 是 老师 吗？

Bú shì, tā shì
B：不是，她是（ ）。

Wǎnshang chī mǐfàn
39．A：晚上 吃 米饭（ ）？

Hǎo, wǎnshang jiàn。
B：好，晚上 见。

Nàge rén jiào shénme
40．A：那个 人 叫 什么（ ）？

Duìbuqǐ, nǐ shuō shéi?
B：对不起，你 说 谁？

Listening Materials

Unit Assesements

Unit 1

1. A：这是哪儿？ B：这是美国。
2. A：你的爸爸是医生吗？ B：不，我的爸爸是老师。
3. A：你的妈妈是老师吗？ B：不，我的妈妈是医生。
4. 你的家在哪儿？
5. 王贝贝是小学生，李心爱是小学生吗？
6. 你爸爸是医生吗？

Unit 2

1. A：很高兴认识你。 B：我也很高兴。
2. A：谢谢你！ B：不客气。
3. A：你是哪国人？ B：我是美国人。
4. Linda是哪国人？
5. 对不起！
6. 谢谢你！

Unit 3

1. A：欢迎你来我们家！ B：谢谢！
2. A：你真漂亮！ B：谢谢，您也很漂亮。
3. A：我们喝牛奶，好吗？ B：好的。
4. 贝贝的妈妈漂亮吗？
5. Tom和贝贝是好朋友吗？
6. 我们吃苹果，好吗？

Unit 4

1. 桌子上有茶。
2. 手里有很多铅笔。
3. 椅子上有书。
4. 这是谁的房间？
5. 房间里面有桌子吗？
6. 这个房间漂亮吗？

Unit 5

1. 我会画画儿。
2. 他会写汉字。
3. 我们学汉语两年了。

4. 你会不会说汉语？
5. 我学习画画儿两个月了。你呢？
6. 中国画漂亮吗？

Unit 6
1. 我们去动物园怎么样？
2. 喂？你好！
3. 王小和的电话是15533026116。
4. 喂？你是李心爱吗？
5. 星期天我们去商店怎么样？
6. 我们在哪儿见？

Unit 7
1. A：现在几点？　B：六点四十分。
2. A：你在哪儿吃饭？　B：我在家吃饭。
3. A：你几点起床？　B：我七点起床。
4. 十点了，睡觉吧！
5. 王贝贝在哪儿学画画？
6. 你今天吃了什么？

Unit 8
1. A：你有没有铅笔？　B：有。
2. A：你有弟弟吗？　B：我有一个弟弟。
3. A：他帅吗？　B：他很帅！
4. 你有没有妹妹？
5. 你有几个好朋友？
6. 你的哥哥怎么样？

Unit 9
1. A：多少钱？　B：二十块。
2. A：你喜欢什么颜色？　B：我喜欢绿色。
3. A：你要买什么？　B：我要买书！
4. 你的桌子是什么颜色的？
5. 你觉得绿色的书包怎么样？
6. 铅笔多少钱？

Unit 10
1. 哥哥比我大三岁。　2. 我觉得水比牛奶好喝。　3. 我比弟弟高。
4. 今天的天气怎么样？　5. 今天比昨天冷吗？　6. 姐姐比你大几岁？

Unit 11

1. 我的头很热。
2. 我们去医院吧。
3. 多喝水！
4. Tom怎么了？
5. 医生说什么？
6. 妈妈的脚怎么样了？

Unit 12

1. 妈妈在做饭呢！
2. 爸爸在看书呢！
3. 我在玩儿呢！
4. 海南在哪儿？
5. 北京比海南冷吗？
6. 你做什么呢？

YCT Friendly Test （Unit1–Unit6）

第一部分

一共5个题，每题听两次。

例如：中国画

对不起

1. 两只小鸟　2. 看书　3. 真漂亮　4. 桌子和椅子　5. 打电话

第二部分

一共5个题，每题听两次。

例如：我的妈妈是医生。

6．书包里面有什么？　7．她是一个小学生。　8．椅子上边有只猫。

9．喝可乐，好吗？　10．这个房间怎么样？

第三部分

一共5个题，每题听两次。

例如：A：你爸爸是老师吗？　B：不。我爸爸是医生。

11．A：她是哪国人？　B：她是中国人。

12．A：你今年几岁了？　B：我今年十岁了。

13．A：这是什么？　B：这是铅笔。

14．A：桌子上边有什么？　B：有书。

15．A：房间里面有什么？　B：有桌子和椅子。

第四部分

一共5个题，每题听两次。

例如：你的家在哪儿？　A 我叫王贝贝。　B 在北京。✓　C 九岁。

16．谢谢你！　A 对不起 。　B 没关系。　C 不客气。

17．心爱来了吗？　A 她是美国人。　B 来了。　C 请坐。

18．你会不会说汉语？　A 好。　B 谢谢。　C 会。

19．我学习中国画两年了，你呢？

A 真漂亮。　B 我学习中国画三个月了。　C 没关系。

20．明天我们去商店，怎么样？

A 我来了。　B 认识你很高兴。　C 好的。

（本套试题由本书作者编写。）

YCT Friendly Test （Unit1–Unit12）

第一部分

一共5个题，每题听两次。

例如：看医生

长头发

1．红苹果　　2．大耳朵　　3．二十八号　　4．很冷　　5．看书

第二部分

一共5个题，每题听两次。

例如：你是红色的，我是黄色的。

6．我现在去商店。

7．看，铅笔在那儿，她的头发上。

8．谁吃了我的香蕉？

9．睡觉了？那好，明天早上见。

10．七点了，我要起床了。

第三部分

一共5个题，每题听两次。

例如：A：他在做什么呢？　B：他？他在睡觉。

11．A：今天星期几？　B：今天？今天星期三。

12．A：那是你的吗？　B：不是，那是我哥哥的。

13．A：高兴吗？　B：高兴，我喜欢在水里玩儿。

14．A：这是谁的手？　B：你说呢？妈妈。

15．A：你好，你喝什么？　B：谢谢，我喝茶。

第四部分

一共5个题，每题听两次。

例如：她是谁？

A 不客气。　B 去医院。　C 我的学生。

16．明天天气热不热？

A 不热。　B 真漂亮。　C 在里面。

17．你爸爸呢？

A 我认识。　B 我妹妹。　C 去学校了。

18．我可以坐这儿吗？

A 谢谢。　B 几个椅子。　C 可以，请坐。

19．你们学校有多少中国学生？

A 中国人。　B 五十多个。　C 我们的朋友。

20．你姐姐会做面条儿吗？

A 她不会。　B 很好吃。　C 买了四个包子。

（本套试题为国家汉办考试处提供的YCT二级考试真题。了解考试详情可登录“汉语考试服务网”：www.chinesetesting.cn）

Word List

Pinyin	Character	Unit
B		
ba	吧（3）	7
bāozi	包子	7
Běijīng	北京	1
bǐ	比	10
búkèqi	不客气	2
C		
chá	茶	4
chuáng	床（4）	4
D		
dǎ diànhuà	打电话	6
dìdi	弟弟	8
diànshì	电视	11
dòngwùyuán	动物园（3）	6
duìbuqǐ	对不起	2
duōshao	多少	9
F		
fángjiān	房间	4
fēnzhōng	分钟	7
H		
Hǎinán	海南（外）	12
Hànyǔ	汉语	5
hǎochī	好吃	2
hóng	红	9
huà	画	5
huānyíng	欢迎（3）	3
huáng	黄	9
huì	会	5
J		
jiǎo	脚	11
juéde	觉得	9
K		
kěyǐ	可以	11
kǒu	口	11
kuài	块	9

Pinyin	Character	Unit
L		
lái	来	3
le	了	5
lěng	冷	10
lǐmiàn	里面	4
liǎng	两	5
líng	零	6
lǜ	绿	9
M		
mǎi	买	9
méi guānxi	没关系	2
méiyǒu	没有	8
mèimei	妹妹	8
míngzi	名字	1
N		
ne	呢	5
nián	年	1
nín	您（3）	3
P		
péngyou	朋友	3
piàoliang	漂亮	3
Q		
qǐchuáng	起床	7
qiānbǐ	铅笔	4
qián	钱	9
qǐng	请	2
R		
rè	热	10
Rìběnrén	日本人（外）	2
S		
shàngbian	上边	4
shū	书	9
shūbāo	书包	4
shuìjiào	睡觉	7
shuài	帅（外）	8

Pinyin	Character	Unit
shuō	说	5
shuōhuà	说话	11
T		
tiānqì	天气	10
tóngxué	同学	2
W		
wán	玩	7
wǎnshang	晚上	7
wèi	喂（3）	6
X		
xiāngjiāo	香蕉	7
xīn	新（3）	2
xióngmāo	熊猫	6
xuésheng	学生	1
xuéxí	学习	5
Y		
yánsè	颜色	9
yào	要	9
yě	也	1
yīshēng	医生	1
yīyuàn	医院	11
yǐzi	椅子	4
Z		
zǎo	早	10
zǎoshang	早上	7
zěnme	怎么	11
zěnmeyàng	怎么样	6
zhāng	张（外）	1
zhēn	真	3
zhī	只	5
zhuōzi	桌子	4
zuótiān	昨天	10
zuò	坐	2
zuò	做	12

注：汉字后括号内的数字“3、4”显示该词在YCT大纲中的级别；“外”表示该词为YCT大纲以外的词汇；没有特别标注的词均为YCT二级词。

Introduction to Youth Chinese Test (YCT)

中小学生汉语考试英文为Youth Chinese Test，简称YCT，是一项国际汉语能力标准化考试，考查汉语非第一语言的中小学生在日常生活和学习中运用汉语的能力。YCT分笔试和口试两部分，笔试和口试是相互独立的。笔试包括YCT（一级）、YCT（二级）、YCT（三级）和YCT（四级）；口试包括YCT（初级）和YCT（中级），采用录音形式。

Youth Chinese Test (YCT), a standardized international Chinese proficiency test, is directed at examining non-native primary and secondary school students' ability to apply Chinese language in their studies and daily lives. It consists of two independent parts: a written test and an oral test. The written test is made up of four levels from YCT-Level 1 to YCT-Level 4. The oral test includes YCT-Speaking (Basic) and YCT-Speaking (Intermediate), and the candidates' on-site performance will be recorded.

考试等级 YCT Levels

等级 Level	词 汇 量 Vocabulary	学习进度参考 Required Preparation (Cumulative Total)
YCT 4	600	按每周2-3课时进度学习汉语二个学期以上 At least two semesters of preparation studying 2-3 hours weekly.
YCT 3	300	按每周2-3课时进度学习汉语二个学期（一学年） Two semesters (one academic year) of preparation, at 2-3 study hours per week.
YCT 2	150	按每周2-3课时进度学习汉语一个学期（半学年） One semester of preparation, at 2-3 study hours per week.
YCT 1	80	按每周2-3课时进度学习汉语3个月 Three months of preparation, at 2-3 study hours per week.
YCT口语中级 YCT-Speaking (Intermediate)	400	按每周2-3课时进度学习汉语两个学期以上 At least two semesters preparation, at 2-3 study hours per week.
YCT口语初级 YCT-Speaking (Basic)	200	按每周2-3课时进度学习汉语一到二个学期 One to two semesters preparation, at 2-3 study hours per week.

通过 YCT（一级）的考生可以理解并使用最常用的汉语词语和句子，具备进一步学习汉语的能力。

通过 YCT（二级）的考生可以理解并使用一些非常简单的汉语词语和句子，满足具体的交际需求。

通过 YCT（三级）的考生可以用汉语就熟悉的日常话题进行简单而直接的交流，达到初级汉语优等水平。

通过 YCT（四级）的考生可以运用汉语完成生活、学习中的基本交际任务，在中国旅游时，可应对遇到的大部分交际任务。

a. YCT- Level 1

Examination candidates who reach YCT-Level 1 can understand and put into practice vocabulary and sentences for daily use and have a foundation to pursue advanced Chinese studies.

b. YCT - Level 2

Examination candidates who reach YCT-Level 2 can understand and use simple words and sentences to accomplish specific communication tasks.

c. YCT-Level 3

Examination candidates who reach YCT-Level 3 can use Chinese language to do simple and direct conversations about familiar daily topic, and achieve excellent level in the primary Chinese.

d. YCT-Level 4

Examination candidates who reach YCT-Level 4 can complete basic communicative tasks in daily life and study, and they can handle most communication tasks they encounter when travelling in China.

试卷结构 Test Paper Structure

笔试科目 Written Test	听力题目 Speaking Questions	阅读题目 Reading Questions	书写题目 Writing Questions	时间（分钟） Duration (min)	总分 Total Score	合格线 Passing Score
YCT 1	20	15		35	200	120
YCT 2	20	20		50	200	120
YCT 3	35	25		60	200	120
YCT 4	40	30	10	85	300	180

口试科目 Oral Test	听后重复 Listen And Repeat	听后回答 Listen And Answer	看图说话 Look And Say	回答问题 Speak Your Answer	时间(分钟) Duration (min)	总分 Total Score	合格线 Passing Score
初级 Basic	15	5	5		17	100	60
中级 Intermediate	10		2	2	19	100	60

YCT的目标 The Objectives of YCT

- 激发和鼓励汉语学习热情
- 提高汉语交际能力
- 培养汉语语感和思维能力
- 建立汉语学习的自信心和荣誉感
- Stimulate more enthusiasm about Chinese learning
- Improve Chinese communication
- Cultivate the sense of Chinese and try to think in Chinese
- Build confidence in learning Chinese

成绩报告 Test Score Report

参加汉语考试的考生皆可获得对应等级的成绩报告。中小学生汉语考试成绩长期有效。可为检测学校汉语课程的教学效果提供参考。

All examination candidates will receive a test score report of their corresponding level. The test score will be kept valid with a long-term certificate. The score report acts as a reference for primary and secondary schools to evaluate their Chinese programs.

汉语考试夏令营 Summer Camp

为激发海外学生学习汉语的积极性，鼓励其踊跃参加汉语考试，汉办从2008年起设立“汉语考试夏令营”项目。凡在海外参加国家汉办各种汉语考试的考生，皆可以申请“汉语考试夏令营”。具体事宜，考生须咨询考点。

To stimulate overseas students to learn Chinese and encourage them to take Chinese tests, HANBAN launches a project, Chinese Test Summer Camp, starting from 2008 onword. All examination candidates who take the above-mentioned tests abroad are eligible to apply for the Chinese Test Summer Camp. For details, please contact the local test center.

资源分享 Resource Sharing

请登陆www.chinesetesting.cn查询更多信息。我们提供大纲和真题集下载、网上报名、成绩报告查询等服务。

报名/成绩查询：kaowu@chinesetesting.cn

综合：kaoshi@hanban.org

Please visit www.chinesetesting.cn for further information. There is both *Test Syllabus* as well as *Official Examiniation Papers* in downloadable on the website. Students can register for the test, view scores and perform other inquiries online.

Registration/Grades: kaowu@chinesetesting.cn

General Inquiries: kaoshi@hanban.org

图书在版编目(CIP)数据

阳光汉语教师手册. 2/(美)刘骏主编. —北京:商务印书馆,2013
ISBN 978-7-100-09500-6

Ⅰ.①阳… Ⅱ.①刘… Ⅲ.①汉语—对外汉语教学—教学参考资料 Ⅳ.①H195.4

中国版本图书馆 CIP 数据核字(2012)第 226302 号

阳光汉语教师手册·2
刘骏〔美〕 主编

商 务 印 书 馆 出 版
(北京王府井大街 36 号 邮政编码 100710)
商 务 印 书 馆 发 行
北京中科印刷有限公司印刷
ISBN 978-7-100-09500-6

2013 年 3 月第 1 版 开本 787×1092 1/16
2013 年 3 月北京第 1 次印刷 印张 9
定价:58.00 元